THE

GARDENER'S YEAR

THE

GARDENER'S YEAR

by

Karel Čapek

illustrated by

Josef Čapek

translated by Geoffrey Newsome

with a foreword by Bel Mooney

A Claridge Press Book

continuum
LONDON • NEW YORK

A translation from the Czech original of Karel Čapek's *Zahradníkův rok* with Josef Čapek's original illustrations. The right of Geoffrey Newsome to be identified as the translator of this work has been asserted by him in accordance with the Copyright, Designs and Patents Act 1998.

Continuum,
The Tower Building,
11 York Road,
London. SE1 7NX
www.continuumbooks.com

First published in Prague in 1929 . First translated into English in 1931.
This edition first published in 2004
Reprinted 2004

Cover illustrations by Josef Čapek

Printed by J. H. Haynes & Co. Ltd. Sparkford, Britain

CIP data for this title is available from the British Library

ISBN: 0826474616 (hbk)

62 illustrations by Josef Čapek, one by Adolf Hoffmeister and one photograph taken by F. Illek.

Literature, Gardening

CONTENTS

$\mathcal{JB}$

FOREWORD

One of our most dedicated gardeners, HRH The Prince of Wales has written: 'For many, the creation of a garden, or the care and nurturing of a garden, is of far greater significance than gardening itself... the garden can become a sanctuary, a place of escape... a glimpse of Paradise; a sacred space where humanity, nature and the Divine meet in harmony.'

It is impossible to separate the spiritual history of humankind from such gardening. Of course, people needed to cultivate for sustenance, but beyond that, what was the point of those tapestries of flowers? To delight the senses, certainly, as in the *Song of Songs*. Yet the ubiquity of the Garden as symbol testifies to its power. The Incas revered the mythical garden of the sun, and in Taoist religion the perfection of miniature gardens reflects Paradise. The four gardens of Paradise in Islam (Soul, Heart, Spirit, Essence) symbolise the mystic journey of the soul. Then in Christian culture the idea of the enclosed garden, the *hortus conclusus* within which is fruitfulness, is emblematic of the Virgin, the Immaculate Conception...

1

What, you may ask, has all this to do with a manual on gardening? The point is, nobody would be interested in Čapek's gentle, witty and profound odyssey through one year within a small territory, were it not for the fact that he is ruminating on the cultivation of far more than flowers. In an era of gardening programmes on television and radio, and many a print supplement, cutting edge gardening lore must surely render Čapek merely quaint. But this text is about transformation through labour, and as such attains the power of myth. Its structure evokes both the delicacy and the realism of a mediaeval Book of Hours: the delicacy in the execution, the realism in the awareness that backbreaking, ritual toil is the only way to attain beauty — and therefore transcendence. It celebrates the perennial miracle: that out of the earth comes forth sweetness — testimony both to the experience and patience of the gardener and the eternal mystery of nature.

Bel Mooney
Spring 2003

2

TRANSLATOR'S NOTE

Karel Čapek's (pronounced 'Chupek') *The Gardener's Year* was first published in an English translation in February, 1931. The translators were the Eton schoolmaster, Robert Weatherall, and his Czechoslovak wife, Marie Isakovicsová. This has been the only translation of the book available in English in either Britain or America for over seventy years. In Britain, it was well received by reviewers and the reading public alike, with five editions being published in the first year alone. Indeed, after a translation of *Letters from England*, it was the bestselling English translation of one of Čapek's books. However, it has not been published in Britain since 1966. In America, the translation is still in print, having been published since 1984 by the University of Wisconsin Press and since 2002 by Modern Library, a division of Random House, Inc.

Otakar Vočadlo, who knew Čapek well and courageously published a book[†] about him and his writings in communist Czechoslovakia, commented in his book

---

[†] Otakar Vočadlo, *Anglické listy Karla Čapka*, Academia, 1975.

3

on some of Čapek's translators into English. While he was critical of Paul Selver, and particularly of Selver's translation of *Letters from England*, he was far more complimentary about the Weatheralls and their translation of *The Gardener's Year*. However, while Vočadlo was undoubtedly right in his assessment of Selver's translation of *Letters from England*, I do not think that one can honestly say that the standard of the Weatheralls' translation of *The Gardener's Year* was any better.

It is for these two reasons — that a translation of *The Gardener's Year* has been unavailable in Britain for so long and that I thought that a better English translation could be written — that I have attempted a new translation of my own. In my own translation I have tried to bring out far more of the original qualities of Čapek's book and I hope that the reader will enjoy these.

Translating a book which is so full of plant names and botanical terms presents obvious challenges. None, though, are any greater than the challenge of doing justice to Čapek's diversity of styles and effects. However, the greatest difficulty which I have encountered has not been one of translating at all but of settling on the most suitable usage when transcribing plant names. I have not found a solution with which I am entirely satisfied and, in case the reader may feel a similar unease, I think that I ought to explain how I settled on my solution.

It is common usage for Latin or 'scientific' plant

4

names to be printed in italic type. The first of these, the generic name, usually has an initial capital letter; the second, the specific or 'trivial' name, usually has a first letter in the lower case. So, for example, it is usual to write *Urtica dioica*. Where a generic name is used without a specific name, this, too, is often printed in italic type with an initial capital letter, as in *Forsythia*. Having accepted these fairly standard typographical conventions, I inevitably felt that, for the sake of textual consistency, English common plant names ought to be printed with their proper capital letters, too, even though such transcription tends to be less common today than it once was. I also felt that giving common plant names their proper capital letters would help to convey something of Čapek's own sense of plants as named characters in a drama. Such transcription does, however, inevitably have its shortcomings. It does mean, for example, that there are occasions when a word like 'Rose' appears with an initial capital letter even though we are more used to seeing it written as 'rose'. It also means that there are instances when, in a list of plant names, some names appear in italic type next to others which do not. I hope that it will now be understood, at least, how such incongruities have — necessarily — come about. I do not believe that they will distract the reader too much from a fluent enjoyment of Čapek's delightful book.

Geoffrey Newsome
Bishop's Cleeve 2003

5

THE

GARDENER'S

YEAR

HOW GARDENS ARE LAID OUT

There are a number of ways of laying out a garden. The best is by taking on a gardener. A gardener will set up all sorts of sticks, twigs and brooms for you which he will insist are Maples, Hawthorns, Elders, standards, half-standards and other natural species. Then he will root about in the earth, turn it over and tamp it down again, make little paths out of rubble, stick some sort of withered leaves in the ground here and there which he will claim are perennials, sow seed for the future lawn which he will call English Ryegrass and Brown Bent, Foxtail Grass, Dogstail and Cat Tail Grass, and afterwards he will depart, leaving behind him a garden which is brown and bare, as it was on the first day of the creation of the world; but he will impress upon you that you will need to water all this soil of the earth carefully every day and that when the grass comes out you will need to have some gravel delivered for the paths. Well, fine.

One would think that watering a garden was an absolutely simple affair, especially if one has a hose. It soon becomes apparent that, until it has been

9

domesticated, a hose is an uncommonly wily, dangerous creature. It writhes, jumps, springs, makes lots of
water underneath itself and plunges lustily into the
mud which it has created; whereupon, it hurls itself at
the person who is intending to do the watering and
entwines itself round his legs. You have to tread on it
and then it rears up and twists itself round your waist
and neck. While the afflicted person is wrestling with
it as though with a python, the monster turns its brass
nozzle upwards and spouts a powerful stream of water
at the windows, on to your freshly hung curtains. You
have to seize it by the head vigorously and stretch it as
long as possible. The beast rages with pain and starts
spraying water not from the head, but from the
hydrant and from somewhere in the middle of its body.
At the first attempt, you need three people to restrain
it to any degree. All three then leave the scene of battle

10

smeared up to the ears in mud and amply watered. As for the garden, in some places it has changed into greasy pools, whereas in others it is cracking with thirst.

If you do this every day, after a fortnight weeds will start to spring up instead of grass. It is one of the mysteries of nature why the most rampant, bristly weeds grow from the best grass seed. Perhaps weed seed should be sown in order for a nice lawn to sprout. After three weeks the lawn is densely overgrown with thistles and other wickednesses, creeping or rooted several feet into the ground. If you try to uproot them, they break off at the root or take whole clods of earth with them. It is like this: the greater the nuisance, the more it thrives.

Meanwhile, by a mysterious transformation of matter, the rubble of the paths has turned into the stickiest, greasiest clay imaginable.

Still, weeds have to be rooted out of the lawn. You weed and weed and behind your steps the future lawn turns into bare, brown earth, as it was on the first day of the creation of the world. Only in two or three places does something like greenish mould break out, something merely suggested, scant, and like down. There is no doubt that it is grass. You tiptoe round it and drive away the sparrows; and while you are gaping at the earth, before you can say 'Jack Robinson', the first small leaves break out on the Gooseberry bushes and Currant bushes. You will never catch sight of the spring.

Your attitude towards things has changed. If it rains, you say that it is raining on the garden. If the sun shines, it is not just shining any old how but shining on the garden. If it is night-time, you are pleased that the garden is resting.

One day, you will open your eyes and the garden will be green, tall grass will be glistening with dew, and swollen, crimson buds will be looking out from a thicket of Rose crowns; and the trees will have aged and will be full and dark with heavy tops and full, decayed scents in the damp shade. And you will not remember the frail, bare, brown garden of these days anymore, the uncertain down of the first grass, the meagre flowering of the first buds or all this clayey, poor, touching beauty of the garden as it has been laid out.

Well, fine; but now you have to water and weed and pick the stones out of the soil.

HOW A GARDENER COMES
INTO BEING

Contrary to all appearances, a gardener is not grown from seed, shoot, bulb, tuber or offset but comes into being through experience, surroundings and natural conditions. When I was little, I had a rebellious, why even malicious, attitude towards my father's garden because I was forbidden from treading on the flowerbeds and plucking the unripe fruit. Likewise, in the Garden of Eden, Adam was prohibited from treading on the borders and plucking the fruit of the Tree of Knowledge because it was not yet ripe, except that Adam — just like us children — did pluck the unripe fruit and, as a result, was expelled from Paradise; from which time on, the fruit of the Tree of Knowledge has been, and always will be, unripe.

When you are in the flower of youth you think that a flower is what you wear in a buttonhole or give to a girl. Somehow you do not properly understand that a flower is something which hibernates, which has to be hoed and manured and watered and transplanted and propagated and pruned and tied back and rid of weeds and fruit spots and dry leaves and greenfly and mildew. Instead of digging over flowerbeds, you chase after girls, indulge your ambition, savour the fruits of life which you have not grown yourself and generally behave completely destructively. A certain ripeness, I would say a certain age of paternity, is needed before a person can become an amateur gardener. Moreover, you need a garden of your own. Usually, you have it done by a professional gardener, thinking that after work you will be able to walk round it, looking at and enjoying the flowers and listening to the twittering of the birds. One day, you will happen to bed in a plant with your own hand; in my case, it was a House Leek. In the process, a bit of soil will get into your body through an agnail or something and will cause a sort of poisoning or inflammation; in short, you will be inflamed into becoming an ardent gardener. Seize but a claw and the whole bird is caught. Another time, a gardener comes into being by being infected by the neighbours. Perhaps he sees a neighbour's Sweet William flowering and he says to himself, 'Dammit, why shouldn't one flower for me too? And we'll see if mine won't be even better!' From these beginnings, the gardener sinks ever deeper into this newly awakened passion, enlivened by new successes and lashed on by new failures. The lust of the collector breaks out in him, driving him on to cultivate everything in the alphabet from *Acaena* to *Zauschneria*. Later, a zeal to specialise develops in him which turns a hitherto sane person into a Rose grower, *Dahlia* grower or other sort of eccentric maniac. Others still fall victim to an artistic passion and continually rearrange, change and

14

redesign their gardens, compose colours, regroup clusters and swap what stands where and what grows where, goaded on by so-called creative discontent. Let no-one think that true gardening is a bucolic, meditative activity: it is an insatiable passion, like everything which the thorough person sets himself to.

I will also tell you how to recognise a true gardener. 'You must come and see me,' he says. 'I want you to see my garden.' When you do go, to please him, you find his rear end protruding somewhere among the perennials. 'I'll be right there,' he says over his shoulder, 'as soon as I've planted this.' 'Don't put yourself out,' you say to him affably. After a while, he has probably planted it. He stands up quickly, dirties your hand and, glowing with hospitality, says, 'Well, come and have a look. I know it's a small garden but — Just a minute,' he says and bends down over a border to weed some blades of grass. 'Well, come on. I'll show you my *Dianthus musalae.* You'll be amazed. Damn, I've forgotten to hoe here,' he says and starts to poke about in the soil. After a quarter of an hour, he draws himself up again. 'Aha,' he says, 'I wanted to show you this Bellflower, *Campanula wilsonae.* It's the prettiest Bellflower that you'll — Hang on, I must just tie back this *Delphinium.*' When he has tied it back, he remembers, 'Why, you wanted to see the Storksbill. Just a minute,' he growls, 'I must just move this *Aster,* it hasn't got enough space here.' At which point you tiptoe away, leaving his rear end protruding among the perennials.

And when you meet him again he will say to you, 'You must come and see me. One of my Pernetiana Roses is in bloom. You haven't seen it yet. So, will you come? But, of course you will!'

So, fine; let us go and see him as the year passes by.

THE GARDENER'S JANUARY

'Not even January is a time of inactivity for the gardener', say the gardening manuals. Certainly not, for in January the gardener mostly

cultivates the weather.

The weather, after all, is a peculiar affair. It is never quite right. The weather always overshoots in one direction or the other. The temperature never hits the hundred-year norm. It is either five degrees above it or five degrees below. The precipitation is either ten millimetres below the norm or twenty millimetres above it. If it is not too dry, it is inevitably too wet.

If even people who otherwise have no concern with it have so many reasons to complain about the weather, then what about the gardener! If too little snow falls, he grumbles, quite justifiably, that nowhere has had enough. If a lot of snow falls, he expresses his grave fear that it will break his conifers and Rhododendrons. If there is no snow, he moans about the destructive black frosts. If a thaw sets in, he curses the insane winds which accompany it with that

17

wicked sound because they scatter his brushwood and other ground cover across the garden and may even, devil take them, break the odd sapling. If the sun dares to shine in January, the gardener clasps his head in his hands for fear that it is going to bring the bushes into sap too early. If it rains, he worries about his little, alpine plants. If it is dry, he thinks with pain of his Rhododendrons and Andromedas. And, after all, it would not be difficult to satisfy him: it would be enough if from the first day to the last day of January there were simply no whole numbers, if it were nine tenths of a degree below zero, if there were one hundred and twenty-seven millimetres of snow (light and, if possible, fresh), if it were mostly cloudy, with no or only mild winds in a westerly direction; and then everything would be fine. But that is it: no-one bothers about us gardeners, and no-one asks us how things ought to be. That is why the world has turned out the way it has.

*

The worst time for the gardener is when black frosts set in. Then the earth stiffens and dries to the bone, deeper day by day and night after night. The gardener thinks of the roots which are freezing in the soil, dead and hard like stone, of twigs benumbed to the pith by the dry, icy wind, and of freezing buds which the plant packed all its goods and chattels into in the autumn. If I thought it would help, I would dress my Holly in my

own coat and put the Juniper in my own trousers. For you, Pontic Azalea, I would take off my shirt. You, Alum Root, I would cover with a hat. And for you, Tickseed, there is nothing left but my socks; you can make do with those.

There are various ruses for getting the better of the weather and bringing about a change to it. For example, whenever I decide to wear the warmest clothes which I possess, a warm spell regularly sets in. Likewise, a thaw sets in when I arrange to go skiing

19

with some friends in the mountains. Even on occasions when someone writes a newspaper article in which he describes the prevailing frosts, the healthily frostbitten faces, the whirl on the ice rinks and other such phenomena, a thaw comes just at the moment when the article is being set in the typesetting room, so that people read it as a tepid rain is falling outside again and the thermometer is showing eight degrees above zero. And of course the reader will say that the newspapers are full of nothing but lies and deceit: 'Don't bother us with your newspapers'. On the other hand, cursing, complaints, exorcisms, sniffling, saying 'brrr' and other incantations have no effect on the weather at all.

*

As far as January vegetation is concerned, the best-known is so-called flowers on the windows. For these to prosper, you need to have at least a bit of water vapour breathed into the room. If the air is completely dry, you will not even grow a paltry needle on the windows, let alone flowers. Moreover, somewhere the window needs to be badly fitting; where the wind whistles through the window, ice-flowers will grow. This is why they prosper more for poor people than for the rich, because the windows of the rich fit better.

Botanically, ice-flowers are distinguished by the fact that they are not flowers at all, but only leaves. These leaves resemble Endives, Parsley and Celery leaves, as

20

well as various thistles from the Cynarocephalae, Carduaceae, Dipsaceae, Acanthaceae, Umbelliferae and other families. One can compare them with species: with Cotton Thistle or 'Scotch Thistle', Carline Thistle, Plume Thistle, *Notabasis*, Sea Holly, Globe Thistle, Bristlethistle, Teasel, Safflower and Bear's Breeches; and also with several other plants whose leaves are prickly, pinnate, dentated, forked, indented, clipped or runcinate. Sometimes they resemble Ferns or Palm leaves, and at other times Juniper needles. However, they do not have flowers.

*

So, 'not even January is a time of inactivity for the gardener,' as the gardening manuals — certainly only as a consolation — insist. In particular, it is apparently possible to work the soil, insofar as the frost apparently makes it crumble. Bang on New Year's Day, therefore, the gardener rushes out into his garden to work the soil. He sets to work on it with a spade. After lengthy exertions, he manages to break his spade against the soil, which is as hard as corundum. He tries with a hoe; if he persists, he breaks its handle in two. He even grabs a pick and manages at least to dig up a Tulip bulb which he had planted in the autumn. The only expedient is to work the soil with a chisel and hammer, except that this is a slow process which soon becomes tiring. Perhaps the soil could be loosened with dynamite, but this is not something which the gardener usually has. Fine, let us leave it to the thaw.

And lo, the thaw arrives and the gardener rushes into the garden to work the soil. After a while, he brings everything that has thawed on the surface into the house, stuck to his boots. Nevertheless, he wears a blissful expression and insists that the ground is opening up. Meanwhile, there is nothing left but to 'do various preparatory jobs for the approaching season'. 'If you have a dry spot in the cellar, prepare some potting soil,

thoroughly mixing leafmould, compost, rotten cow dung and a little sand.' Excellent! Except that there are coke and coal in the cellar. These women spread everywhere with their daft, domestic necessities. Well then, there ought to be enough space in the bedroom for a nice little heap of humus —

'Use the wintertime to repair your pergola, arbour or summerhouse.' Well and good, except that I do not happen to have a pergola, arbour or summerhouse. 'Even in January it is possible to lay turf'. If only I knew where.

Perhaps in the hallway or in the attic. 'Above all, keep watch on the temperature in the greenhouse.' Well, I would gladly keep watch, but I have not got a greenhouse. These gardening manuals do not tell you much.

*

And so, wait, wait! God above, how long January is! If only it were February already.

'Because something can be done in the garden in February?'

'Why, yes; maybe even in March.'

And meanwhile, without him having an inkling, and without him having taken the least effort towards it, Crocuses and Snowdrops have sprung up in the garden.

SEEDS

Some people say that charcoal should be added to it, whereas others contest this. Some recommend a bit of yellow sand because it apparently contains iron, while others caution against this for the simple reason that it apparently contains iron. Others still recommend pure river sand, others only peat, and yet others sawdust. In short, preparing soil for seeding is a great mystery and a magical ritual. Marble dust should be added to it (but where to find some?), three-year-old cow dung (here it is not clear whether it should be dung from three-year-old cows or a three-year-old heap), a sprinkle of fresh molehill, clay pounded to dust from old, adobe bricks, sand from the Elbe (but not from the Vltava), three-year-old hotbed soil, and perhaps also some humus from Golden Ferns and a handful of soil from the grave of a hanged maiden. All of this should be properly mixed (gardening books do not say whether by the new moon or full moon or on Walpurgis Night), and when you pour this mysterious soil into flowerpots (soaked in water which has been standing in the sun for three years, on the bottom of which you put boiled crocks and a piece of charcoal, which other authorities of course decry), when, then, you have accomplished all of this, so observing the hundreds of prescriptions, mainly differing from each other, which make this ritual so exceedingly difficult, you can proceed to the heart of the matter, namely, to sowing seeds.

As far as seeds are concerned, there are some which are similar to snuff, some to light, blond nits and others to glossy, crimson-black fleas without legs; some are flat like small coins, others are plumply rounded, others are thin like small needles, winged, prickly, downy, bare and hairy, as large as a cockroach and as minute as sunlit dust. I can vouch for it that each kind is different and each one is odd: life is complex. From this large, crested monster a small, low, dry thistle is supposed to grow; whereas from this yellow nit a huge, fat *Cotyledon* is apparently going to emerge. What am I supposed to do? I simply do not believe it.

All right, have you finished sowing? Have you put the flowerpots in tepid water and covered them with glass? Have you covered the windows against the sun and closed them so that you can produce a forty-degree, hotbed heat in the room? Well, fine; now begins the great, feverish activity of every seed grower, namely, waiting. Drenched in sweat, without a coat, without a waistcoat and without a breath, the expectant gardener bends over his flowerpots and with his eyes draws up the shoots which are supposed to be emerging.

26

On the first day, nothing yields and the waiting person tosses and turns in his bed at night, unable to wait till morning.

On the second day, the mysterious soil reveals a wisp of mould. The waiting person rejoices that this is the first sign of life.

On the third day, something creeps up on a long, white leg and grows like crazy. The waiting person almost exults out loud that it is here at last and tends the first seedling as though it were the apple of his eye.

On the fourth day, when the shoot has by now protruded to an impossible length, a worry rises in the waiting person that it might be a weed. It soon becomes apparent that this anxiety was not without cause. The first, long, thin thing which grows in a flowerpot is always a weed. Evidently, it is some sort of law of nature.

Well then, some time on the eighth day or even later, quite out of the blue, at some mysterious and unobserved moment (for no-one has ever seen it or caught it out), the soil very quietly pushes apart and the first shoot appears. I always thought that a plant grows from either the seed downwards, like a root, or from the seed upwards, like the haulm of a potato. Let me tell you that it is not like that. Almost every plant grows under the seed upwards, lifting its seed on its head like a cap. Just imagine if a child were to grow, carrying its mother on its head. It is simply a marvel of nature; and almost every shoot performs this athletic trick. It lifts the seed with an ever more daring

27

raising until one day it drops it or throws it away; and now it stands here, bare and fragile, plump or pinched, and has two quite ludicrous little leaves on top and between these two leaves something will later appear—

But just what, I will not tell you yet; I have not got that far yet. They are only two, small leaves on a small, pale leg, but it is so strange, it is capable of so many variations, it is different with every plant. What did I want to say? Oh, I know, nothing; or only that life is more complex than anyone can imagine.

THE GARDENER'S FEBRUARY

In February, the gardener continues with his January work, especially in as far as mostly cultivating the weather goes. For, you should know, February is a dangerous time which threatens the gardener with black frosts, sun, damp, drought and wind. This shortest month, this whippersnapper among months, this premature, leap-year and altogether unsound month surpasses all the others in its cunning tricks; beware of it. By day it wheedles buds out of the bushes and at night it scorches them; with one hand it is pleasant to us and with the other it snaps its fingers under our nose. The devil only knows why in leap years one day is added to precisely this fickle, catarrhal, crafty runt of a month. In a leap year, a day ought to be added to the beautiful month of May so that there would be thirty-two of them, and that would be fine. What have we gardeners done to deserve this?

Another seasonal job in February is hunting for the first signs of spring. The gardener does not set great store by the first cockchafer or butterfly which usually ushers in the spring in the newspapers; for one thing,

29

he is not at all keen on cockchafers and, for another, the first butterfly is usually the last one from the year before which has forgotten to die. The first signs of spring which the gardener hunts for are less misleading. They are:

1. Crocuses, which spring up in his grass like plump, ready-formed, little spikes. One day, a spike

cracks (as yet no-one has ever witnessed this) and makes a sort of tuft of beautifully green leaves; and this is the first sign of spring. Then:

2. Gardening price lists, which the postman brings. Although the gardener knows them all from memory (just as the *Iliad* begins with the words Ἀμηνιν αειδε, Θεα, so these catalogues begin with the words *Acaena, Acantholimon, Acanthus, Achillea, Aconitum, Adenophora, Adonis* and so on, which every gardener can reel off in his sleep), still he carefully reads through them from *Acaena* to *Wahlenbergia* or *Yucca,* enduring the difficult struggle of deciding what else he ought to order.

3. Snowdrops are another herald of the spring. First, they are sort of pale-green points peeping from the soil; then, they split into two, fat, uterine leaves, and that is that. Then they flower some time at the beginning of February and, I tell you, no Palm of Victory or Tree of Knowledge or Laurel of Glory is more beautiful than this little, white, fragile cup on a pale stalk waving in the rough wind.

4. Neighbours are likewise an unmistakable sign of spring. As soon as they turn out in their gardens with spades, hoes, shears, bast, paint for the trees and all sorts of powders for the soil, the experienced gardener recognises that spring is approaching; and he will put on some old trousers and turn out in the garden with

31

a spade and a hoe so that his own neighbours will recognise that spring is approaching and will convey the joyous news over the fence.

The soil opens up, but does not yet bear a single, green leaf; as yet, it can still be taken in its essence, as a bare, expectant soil. This is the time again for all that manuring and digging, trenching or tranching, and loosening and mixing of the soil. It is now that the gardener discovers that his soil is too heavy, too sticky or too sandy, too acid or too dry. In short, a passion bursts out in him to improve it somehow. You know, soil can be improved using a thousand substances; unfortunately, the gardener does not usually have them to hand. In town, it is somewhat difficult to have pigeon droppings at home, beech leaves, rotten cow manure, old plaster, old peat, ripe turf, mouldering molehills, humus from the woods, river sand, mor, mud from a fish pond, soil from the heaths, charcoal, wood ash, powdered bones, horn shavings, old dung water, horse muck, lime, sphagnum, rot from tree stumps and other life-giving, powdered and wholesome substances, not to mention a good dozen nitrogenous, magnesium, phosphate and other assorted fertilizers.

It is true that there are times when the gardener would like to cultivate, dig over and compost all of these noble soils, ingredients and manures; unfortunately, there would not be space left in the garden then for flowers. So, he improves the soil at least as well as he can. At home, he searches for eggshells, burns bones left from lunch, sets aside his nail clippings, sweeps up soot from the chimney, picks sand out of the sink, skewers lovely horse dung in the street with his stick and carefully digs all of this into his soil; for these are loosening, warm and fertilizing substances. Everything that exists is either good for the soil or not. It is only cowardly shame which prevents the gardener from going into the street to collect what the horses have scattered about; but when he sees a nice pile of manure in the gutter, he does at least sigh at what a waste this is of God's bounty.

33

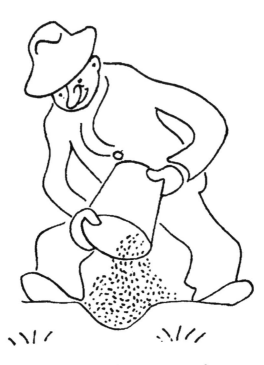

When one just thinks of a mountain of manure in a farmyard! Oh, I know that there are all sorts of powders in tin cans; you can buy whatever you like, all sorts of salts, extracts, slag and meal; you can inoculate the soil with bacteria; you can cultivate it in a white coat, like an assistant at a university or at the chemist. You can do all of this, urban gardener; but when you just think of a fat, brown mountain of manure in a farmyard!

34

But, so that you know, the Snowdrops are already flowering; the Witch-hazels are flowering with their little, yellow stars, and the Hellebores are bearing fat buds; and if you look properly (you must hold your breath as you do), you will find buds and sprouts on almost everything; with a thousand, tiny pulses life is rising from the soil. We gardeners do not give in now; we are rushing into new sap.

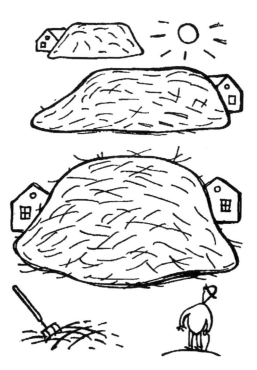

ON THE ART OF GARDENING

When I was only a distant, scatterbrained observer of the finished work of gardens, I thought of gardeners as individuals of a particularly poetic and gentle spirit who cultivated the fragrances of flowers, listening to the singing of the birds. Now, when I look at the matter from a greater proximity, I find that a true amateur

gardener is not someone who cultivates flowers; he is a man who cultivates soil. He is a creature who digs his hands into the earth and leaves a spectacle for us gaping ne'er-do-wells to wonder what is there. He lives submerged in the ground. He builds his memorial in a pile of compost. If he were to go to the Garden of Eden, he would sniff intoxicatedly and say, 'There's humus here, by God!' I think that he would forget to eat the fruit of the tree of the knowledge of good and evil; more likely, he would look to see how he could take away the odd wheelbarrowful of the Lord's paradisiacal topsoil. Or he would discover that the tree of the knowledge of good and evil did not have a nice, bowl-shaped border fashioned round it and would begin to fumble about in the soil, not even knowing what was hanging above his head. 'Adam, where are you?' the Lord would call. 'In a moment,' the gardener would reply over his shoulder, 'I haven't got time just now.' And he would go on making his border.

If gardening man had originated from the beginning of the world by natural selection, he would obviously have evolved into some sort of invertebrate. What possible use does a gardener have for a back? Apparently only for straightening up every so often, saying, 'My back aches!' As regards legs, they can be folded up in all sorts of ways; it is possible to squat, kneel, force your legs somehow underneath you or, lastly, put them behind your neck; fingers are good dibbers for making hollows, palms can crush small clods or part the soil, while the head serves for holding a pipe; only the back

remains an intractable thing which the gardener tries in vain to bend suitably. The garden earthworm does not have a back either. The amateur gardener usually ends with his backside up in the air, his legs and arms straddled, and his head somewhere between his knees, like a grazing mare. He is not a man who would want to 'add even only one cubit to his stature'; on the contrary, he folds his stature in half, squats and makes himself shorter in every possible way. When you see him, he rarely measures more than three feet tall.

Cultivating soil consists, on the one hand, of all manner of digging, hoeing, turning over, filling in, loosening, levelling, smoothing and dressing, and, on the other, of ingredients. No pudding can be more complicated than the preparation of garden soil. As far as I

38

have been able to observe, dung is put into it, manure, guano, leafmould, turf soil, topsoil, sand, straw, lime, kainite, Thomas phosphate, baby powder, saltpetre, horn, phosphates, droppings, ordure, ash, peat, compost, water, beer, knocked-out smoking pipes, charred matches, dead cats, and many other substances. All of this is constantly mixed, dug in and seasoned. As I said, the gardener is not someone who sniffs at a Rose but someone who is persecuted by the idea that 'that soil could do with a bit more lime' or that it is heavy (like lead, the gardener says) and 'could do with some more sand'. Gardening becomes a rather scientific affair. These days, a girl would not be allowed to sing just, 'Underneath our windows a Rose bloom grows'. More likely, she should sing that underneath our windows saltpetre and Beech ashes should be sprinkled and carefully mixed with finely chopped straw. A Rose bloom is, so to speak, only for dilettanti; the gardener's pleasure is rooted deeper, down to the womb of the soil. After death, the gardening enthusiast does not become a butterfly, drunk on the fragrances of flowers, but an earthworm, sampling all the dark, nitrogenous and spicy delights of the soil.

Now, in early spring keen gardeners are, as they say, irresistibly drawn to their gardens; they barely put down their spoon before they are in their borders, lifting their rears to the magnificent, azure sky; here they crush a warm clod between their fingers, here they push a mouldering, priceless piece of last year's manure nearer to the roots, there they wrench a weed

out, and here they pick out a stone; now they ruffle the soil round the Strawberries and, before long, they bow down to some young Lettuces, their nose to the ground, lovingly tickling a delicate wad of roots. In this

position they delight in the spring, while above their loins the sun runs its illustrious course, clouds drift and heavenly birds mate. The Cherry buds are opening now, young leaves are unfurling with a lovely tenderness and blackbirds are shrieking like lunatics; at this point, the true gardening fanatic straightens himself out, stretches his back and says gloomily, 'In the autumn I'll manure it well and add a pinch of sand.'

But there is one moment when the keen gardener draws himself up and unfurls himself to his full height. This is that afternoon hour when he administers the sacrament of water to his garden. At this time, he stands, straight and almost majestic, directing a jet of water from the mouth of a hydrant. The water sparkles in a silver, melodious shower, a balmy breath of dampness wafts from the loose earth, and every leaf is immediately wildly green and sparkles with delectable joy, so that it is almost good enough to eat. 'There, it's had enough now,' the gardener whispers blissfully, by which he does not mean the Cherry tree lathered in buds or the purple Currant bush: he is thinking of the brown soil of the earth.

And when the sun sets, he says with the height of satisfaction, 'I've really toiled today!'

THE GARDENER'S MARCH

If we are to describe the gardener's March according to the truth and age-old experience, we must above all carefully distinguish two things: a) what the gardener should and wants to do, and b) what he really does, not being able to do more.

a) So, it goes without saying what he wants ardently and earnestly: he just wants to remove the brushwood and uncover the plants, dig, manure, make ditches, hoe, dig over, loosen, rake, level, water, propagate, take cuttings, prune, plant, transplant, tie back, spray, fertilize, twine, fill out, sow, sweep, trim, drive off sparrows and blackbirds, sniff the soil, unearth buds with his finger, rejoice at the flowering Snowdrops, wipe off sweat, straighten his back, eat like a wolf and drink like a fish, go to bed with a spade and get up with the lark, glorify the sun and the heavenly drizzle, finger hard buds, cultivate the first spring calluses and blisters, and generally live the gardener's life, broadly, fully and invigoratingly.

b) Instead, he curses because the soil is still frozen or has frozen again, rages in the house like a captive lion in a cage when his garden gets snowed up, sits by the stove with a cold, has to go to the dentist, has a hearing in court, receives a visit from his aunt, great-grandson or the devil's own grandmother and generally loses day after day, persecuted by all sorts of bad

weather, blows of fate, business and adversities which, as luck would have it, crowd in on him in the month of March. For, you know, 'March is the busiest month in the garden, which has to be prepared for the arrival of spring.'

Yes, only as a gardener does man appreciate those somewhat outworn sayings like 'implacable winter', 'fierce north wind', 'savage frost' and other such, poetic railings. Why, he himself uses even more poetic expressions, saying that the winter this year is mon-

44

strous, confounded, darned, wretched, deuced and devilish. Unlike poets, he does not just rail against the north wind but against the maleficent east winds too; and he execrates the raw snowstorm less than the pussyfooting, devious, black frost. He is inclined to figurative sayings such as 'winter resists the assaults of spring' and feels extremely humiliated that in this fight there is no way that he can help overthrow and finish off this tyrannical winter. If he could attack it with a

hoe or a spade, a gun or a halberd, he would gird himself and go into battle, uttering a victorious war cry;
but he cannot do more than wait by his radio every
evening for war reports from the Meteorological Office,
savagely blaspheming against the region of high pres-
sure over Scandinavia or the deep disturbances over
Iceland; for we gardeners know which way the wind
blows.

For us gardeners, folk weatherlore has an urgent
validity too; we still believe that 'St. Matthias cuts the
ice' and if he does not, we expect St. Joseph, heavenly
hatchet man, to cut it. We know that 'in March we
creep behind the hearth' and even believe in Jack
Frost, the spring equinox, St. Swithin's Day, and other
such predictions, from which it is clear that people
from time immemorial have had lousy experiences
with the weather. It would be no surprise if it were said
that 'on the first of May roof-snow melts away', or that
'on St. John of Nepomuk's Night hands and noses get
frostbite', or that 'on St. Peter's and St. Paul's let's wrap
up in our shawls', that 'on St. Methodius's and St.
Cyril's water freezes in the wells', and that 'on St.
Wenceslas's one winter ends and another descends'. In
short, folk weatherlore prophesies mostly inauspi-
cious, dismal things for us. And, therefore, you should
know that the existence of gardeners who, despite
these lousy experiences with the weather, welcome and
usher in the spring year after year, testifies to the indestructible and miraculous optimism of humankind.

*

A person who has become a gardener delights in consulting Old Campaigners. These are elderly and somewhat absentminded people who say every spring that they cannot remember another spring like it. If it is chilly, they declare that they cannot remember such a cold spring: 'Once, it's going on sixty years now, it was so warm that Violets were flowering at Candlemas.' On the other hand, if it is a little warmer, the Campaigners

insist that they cannot remember such a warm spring:
'Once, it's going on sixty years now, we went sledging
on St. Joseph's Day.' In short, even from the testimony
of Old Campaigners it is clear that, as far as the
weather is concerned, an unbridled capriciousness
holds sway in our climate and there is simply nothing
that we can do about it.

No, there is nothing that we can do; it is mid-March
and snow is still lying on the frozen garden. God be
merciful to the gardeners' plants.

I will not divulge to you the secret of how gardeners
recognise each other, whether by smell, some code-
word or a secret sign; but the fact is that they do recognise each other straightaway, be it in the lobby of a theatre, at tea or in the dentist's waiting-room. The first
sentence which they utter will exchange their opinions
about the weather ('No, sir, I can't remember another
spring like it'), at which they will proceed to the ques-
tion of the humidity, to Dahlias, artificial fertilizers, a
type of Dutch Lily ('confounded thing, what's it called
again? Well, it doesn't matter, I'll let you have a bulb'),
to Strawberries, American price lists, the damage
which this year's winter wreaked, scutellar aphids,
Asters, and other, similar themes. They only look as
though they are two men in evening dress in the corri-
dor of a theatre; in a deeper and truer reality, they are
two gardeners with a spade or a watering can in their
hand.

*

When your watch stops, you take it to pieces and then take it to the watchmaker. When someone's car stops, he jacks up a wheel and pokes his finger into it, after which he calls a mechanic. With everything in the world there is something that you can do, everything can be mended and reformed, but there is nothing that you can do about the weather. No zeal or delusions of grandeur, no gimmicks, busybodying or blaspheming will help. A shoot will open out and a bud will sprout when its time and law are met. Here with humility you

49

recognise the impotence of man; you understand that patience is the mother of wisdom.

After all, there is nothing else that you can do.

BUDS

Today, 30th March, at ten o'clock in the morning, the first little *Forsythia* flower opened out behind my back. For three days I had been keeping a watch on its largest shoot, similar to a minute, golden pod, so as not to miss this historic moment; it happened as I was looking at the sky to see if it was going to rain. Tomorrow, the *Forsythia* twigs will be spangled with golden stars. It cannot be held back. The Lilacs, needless to say, have hurried the most; before you can say 'Jack Robinson', they have made slender, fragile little leaves. My friend, you will never keep watch on a Lilac. The Golden Currant is opening out its serrated, pleated ruffs too; but the other bushes and trees are still waiting for some imperious 'Now!' which will breathe from the earth or the sky; and at that moment all the buds will unfurl and it will be here.

Such burgeoning belongs to the phenomena which we humans call 'the march of nature'; but then germination really is a march. Decay is a march of nature too, but it does not at all remind us of a nice, military march; I would not want to compose a 'tempo di marcia' for the march of decay. But if I were a musician, I would write a 'march of the buds'. First, a light march of Lilac battalions would set off; then columns of Currants would begin to march; into this, a heavier parade of Pear and Apple buds would break in, while young grass would strum and twitter on every string which I could muster. And, during this orchestral accompaniment, regiments of well-disciplined buds would march, driving forward without a moment's rest, in 'a magnificent pageant', as they say of military parades. Left, right; left, right. Heavens, what a march!

It is said that in early spring nature turns green; this is not entirely true for it also turns red with crimson and pink buds. There are buds which are dark purple and flushed with numbing cold; others are brown and sticky like pitch; others are whitish like the felt on a doe rabbit's belly; but they can also be mauve and blond or dark like old leather. From some of them an uneven lace is wrung, others are similar to fingers or tongues, and others still resemble nipples. Some swell fleshily, overgrown with down and plump like puppies; others are tightened into a slim, rigid tip; others open with puffed-up, fragile, little tails. I tell you, buds are just as odd and varied as leaves or flowers. A person is never done with discovering the differences. But you have to select a small patch of ground before you can find them. If I hurried on foot as far as Benešov, I would see a smaller piece of spring than if I squatted down in my garden. You must stop; and then you will see parted lips and furtive glimpses, delicate fingers and raised weapons, the delicacy of an infant and the rebellious upsurge of the will to life; and then you will hear the hushed roar of an endless march of buds.

So, while I have been writing this it seems that that mysterious 'Now!' has descended; buds which in the morning were still wreathed in rigid swathing bands have thrown out fragile leaf tips, the *Forsythia* twigs have started to glow with golden stars, budding Pear shoots have spread a little, and golden-green eyes are sparkling on the tips of I do not know what sort of buds. Young verdure is protruding from pitchy scales, fat buds have burst and a filigree of notches and pleats is breaking out of them. Do not be shy, blushing leaf; open out, folded fan; stretch yourself, downy sleeper; the order to start out has been given. Start, preludes of the unwritten march! Gleam in the sun, golden brass; roll, timpani; pipe, flutes; pour out your shower, numberless violins; for the silent, brown, green, little garden has set out on its triumphal march.

THE GARDENER'S APRIL

April is the gardener's true, blessed month. Let lovers go hang with their exaltation of May; in May, trees and flowers only blossom and bloom but in April, they sprout. You should know that this sprouting and germination, these shoots, buds and sprouts are the greatest wonder of nature, and I will not divulge one more word about them. Squat down and rake with nothing but a finger in the loose earth, holding your breath because your said finger is touching a fragile, full shoot. One cannot describe it, just as one cannot describe kisses in words and a few other things.

But while we are on the subject of this fragile shoot, it must be admitted that no-one knows how it comes about but it does happen strikingly often that when you tread on a flowerbed to pick up a dried twig or to weed a devil of a Dandelion, you usually tread on the shoot of a Lily or a Globeflower beneath the surface; so, it cracks under your foot and you freeze with shame and fear; at that moment, you think of yourself as a monster under whose hooves the grass will not grow. Or with infinite care you loosen the soil in a

flowerbed, with the guaranteed result that you hack a budding bulb with your hoe or smoothly slice some *Anemone* sprouts with your spade; starting back in alarm, you crush a flowering *Primula* with your paw or break the young tail of a *Delphinium*. The more scrupulously and carefully you work, the more damage you cause; only years of experience teach you the mystical, rough certainty of the true gardener who treads where God pleases and yet treads

nothing underfoot; and when he does, at least he does not make a fuss about it. Well, only momentarily.

*

Apart from germination, April is also the month for planting. With enthusiasm, yes, with wild enthusiasm

56

and impatience, you have ordered seedlings from the nurseryman without which you could not go on living; you have promised all your gardening friends that you will come to them for cuttings; never, I say, do you have enough with what you have already got. And so, one day, some hundred and seventy seedlings congregate at your house which need to be planted; at that moment, you look round your little garden and find with overwhelming certainty that you have nowhere to put them.

So, the gardener in April is someone who walks round his garden twenty times with a wilting seedling in his hand, trying to find an inch of soil where nothing else is growing. 'No, it's no good here,' he growls quietly. 'I've got those damned Chrysanthemums here; here the Phlox would choke it, and there's a Sweet William here, devil take it. Hmm, the Bellflower has gone and spread out on me here, and there's no space by this Tansy either — where am I going to put it? Hang on, here — no, there's a Monk's-hood here. Or here — but there's a Cinquefoil here. Here would be all right, but it's full of Spiderworts; and here — what's this coming up? I wish I knew. Aha, there's a little bit of space here; hang on, seedling,.I'll bed you down here right away. There you are, you see; and now with God's grace, grow!'

Yes, but two days later the gardener finds that he has planted it right on top of some purple-sprouting Evening Primroses.

*

Gardening man certainly originated by culture and not by natural evolution. If he had originated naturally, he would look different; he would have legs like a beetle so that he would not need to squat, and he would have wings, firstly for their beauty and, secondly, so that he could hover over his borders. Those who have not tried can have no conception of how legs get in a person's way when you have got nothing to stand on; how

unnecessarily long they are when you need to fold them under you and poke a finger in the soil; how impossibly short they are when you need to reach the other side of a flowerbed without treading on a pillow of *Pyrethrum* or a budding Columbine. Or to be hung in a sling and dangle over your flora, or at least have four hands and on them a head and a cap and nothing else, or to have telescopic limbs like a

photographer's tripod! But since the gardener is out-
wardly just as maladapted as the rest of you, there is
nothing left for him but to show what he can do; to balance on the tip of one foot, to float like an imperial
ballerina, to straddle four metres in width, to tread as
gently as a butterfly or a wagtail, to get into a square

inch of soil, to hold his balance against all laws concerning inclining bodies, to reach everywhere and avoid everything and at the same time try to maintain a certain dignity so that people will not laugh at him.

Of course, at a distant, fleeting glance, you will not see any more of a gardener than his rear end; everything else, like his head, arms and legs, is simply beneath him.

*

Thank you for asking, there is going to be masses of it now: Daffodils, Hyacinths and Bunch-flowered Narcissi, Horned Violets and Navelwort, Saxifrage, *Draba* and Rockcress and *Hutchinsia* and Primroses and Spring Heather, and whatever out of this lot flowers tomorrow or the day after will make you gape.

*

Of course, anyone can gape. 'Wow, that's a pretty little bunch of lilac-coloured flowers,' says your layman, to which the gardener, a little offended, says, 'Actually, it's *Petrocallis pyrenaica.*' For the gardener is particular about names. A flower without a name is, to put it platonically, a flower without a metaphysical idea. In short, it does not have that true, authentic reality. A nameless flower is a weed; a flower with a Latin name is somehow elevated to the status of an expertise. If a Nettle grows in your flowerbed, stick the label '*Urtica*

61

dioica' on it and you will start to value it; why, you will even loosen the soil for it and manure it with caliche. If you are speaking to a gardener, always ask him, 'What's this Rose called?' 'It's 'Burmeester van Tholle',' the gardener will tell you with pleasure, 'and this is 'Mme. Claire Mordier',' and in this way he will think of you that you are a decent, educated person. And do not take chances with names yourself; do not say, for example, 'Your *Arabis* is flowering well here,' when the gardener can then boom at you angrily, 'As a matter of fact, it's *Schievereckia bornmülleri!*' True, it does not make much difference, but a name is a name, and we gardeners set great store by good names. For this reason, we also hate children and blackbirds, because they pull out and mix up our label pegs; then we happen to point out with surprise, 'Look, this *Laburnum* here is flowering just like Edelweiss — maybe it's some sort of local variation; and it's definitely a *Laburnum* because there's my label next to it.'

FESTIVAL

But I will purposely sing the praises not of the festival of labour but of the festival of private property; and if it does not rain straightaway I will certainly celebrate it now by squatting down and saying, 'Hang on, I'll give you a bit of peat, and I'll cut off this sucker for you; and you'd like to go deeper into the ground, wouldn't you?' And the Aubrietia will say that it would, and I will plant it deeper in the ground. For this is my soil, sprinkled with sweat and blood, literally, for when one cuts off a twig or a shoot, one almost always cuts a finger, which is also just a twig or a shoot. A person with a garden becomes irrevocably a private proprietor; then it is not a Rose that is growing in it, but his Rose; then he does not see and state that the Cherry trees are already blossoming, but that his Cherry trees are blossoming. A person who is a proprietor assumes a certain mutuality with his neighbours, for example as regards the weather; now he says that 'we're not supposed to get any rain' or that 'we've had a good soaking'. In addition, he acquires a no less strong sort of exclusivity; he discovers that his neighbour's trees

63

are sticks and brooms compared with his, or he sees that that Quince would do better in his garden than in his neighbour's, and so on. It is true, therefore, that private property brings out certain class and collective instincts, as, for example, regards the weather; but it is equally true that it awakens terribly strong instincts of selfishness, private enterprise and ownership. There is no doubt that a man would go to war for his beliefs, but more willingly and ferociously still would he go to war for his bit of garden. A person who is the owner of several yards of soil and grows something on them really does become a rather conservative creature, for he is dependent on thousand-year-old laws of nature; do what he may, no revolution can hasten the time of germination and make the Lilac bloom before May; in this, then, a person becomes wise and surrenders to law and custom.

For you, alpine Bellflower, I'll dig a deeper bed. Work! Even this fiddling about in the soil can be called work, for, I tell you, you strain your back and knees doing it. However, it is not for the sake of work, but for the Bellflower; you do not do work because work is beautiful or because it is ennobling or because it is healthy, you do it to make the Bellflower bloom and the Saxifrage grow into a pillow. If you wanted to celebrate something, you would not celebrate this work of yours, but the Bellflower or Saxifrage for which you were doing it. And if instead of writing articles and books you stood at a loom or a lathe, you would not do this work because it was work, but because you would have

64

smoked meat and peas from it or because you have got loads of children and you want to live. And this is why you should celebrate smoked meat and peas today, children and life, everything which you buy through your work and that you pay for through your work. Or you should celebrate what you produce by your work. Road menders should not just celebrate their work, but the roads which have grown from it; and textile workers on the day of the festival of labour should, above all, celebrate the miles of drill and rough cotton which they have extracted from their machines. It is called the festival of labour and not the festival of achievement; and yet one should be prouder of what one has achieved than of the fact that one has simply worked at all.

I asked someone who had visited the late lamented Tolstoy what the boots were like which Tolstoy had stitched himself. Apparently, they were abominable. If someone does a job, he should do it either because he enjoys it or because he is good at it or, lastly, to earn a living; but to stitch boots as a matter of principle, to work as a matter of principle and as a virtue is to do a job which does not count for much. I would expect the festival of labour to reach its peak in a glorification of the human aptitude and know-how which those people command who can take work in the right way. If today we celebrated the bright sparks and sterling fellows of all countries, this day would turn out to be especially merry; it would be a real festival, a pilgrimage day of life, a festival of all good chaps.

Fine, but this festival of labour is a strict and serious day. Don't you worry about it, little, spring Phlox, and open out your first, pink calyx.

THE GARDENER'S MAY

Hey, with all our concern about hoeing and digging, planting and cutting we have not yet got round to the gardener's greatest delight and most intimate pride: his rock garden or 'alpine' rockery. It is obviously called an alpine rockery because this bit of garden allows its keeper to perform breakneck alpinism. If, for example, he wants to plant this tiny little *Androsace* between these two rocks, he has to stand lightly on one foot, here on this rock which is a bit wobbly, and with the other balance majestically in the air so as not to trample on the little cushion of *Erysimum* or the flowering Aubrietia; he has to employ the most fearless straddles, knee bends, backward bends, positions, postures, hops, lunges, forward bends, holds and exercises in order to plant, hoe, dibble and weed among the picturesquely arranged and not altogether firmly seated rocks in his rockery.

From this perspective, cultivating a rockery can be seen to be an exciting and lofty sport. Moreover, it provides you with innumerable fervid surprises as when, for example, at the giddy height of a yard and a half,

you find a flowering tuft of bright, white Edelweiss in your rockery or glacial Clove Pinks or other, as they say, children of the high alpine flora. But what can I tell you? Whoever has not carefully reared these various miniature Bellflowers, Saxifrages, Campions, Speedwells, Sandworts, Drabas and Iberises and Madworts and Phloxes (and Dryases and Erysimums and House Leeks and Stone Crops) and Lavender and

68

Cinquefoil and *Anemone* and Corn Camomile and
Rockcress (and *Gypsophila* and *Edrianthus* and
assorted Thymes) (and *Iris pumila* and *Hypericum
olympicum* and Orange Hawkweed and Rock Rose and
Gentian and *Cerastium* and Common Thrift and
Toadflax) (not forgetting, of course, *Aster alpinus*,
Creeping Wormwood, Fairy Foxglove, Spurge, Soapwort
and Storksbill and *Hutchinsia* and *Paronychia* and
Thlaspi and *Aethionema*, nor of course Snapdragon,
Ladies' Tobacco and countless other exquisite little
plants such as *Petrocallis, Lithospermum, Astragalus*
and others no less important such as Primroses,
alpine Violets and others), well, whoever has not cultivated all these tender plants, not including many
others (of which I will mention at least *Onosma,
Acaena*, Wild Geranium, *Bahia* and *Sagina* and
Cherleria), let him not speak of all the beauties of the
world, for he has not seen the sweetest that this
rugged earth has created in a brief moment of fond-
ness (which has lasted but a few hundred thousand
years). If only you could see a little cushion of
Dianthus musalae strewn with the pinkest little flowers that ever —

But what can I tell you? Only cultivators of rock-
eries know this sectarian rapture.

Yes, for the cultivator of a rockery is not only a gardener but a collector, which ranks him among the
most serious maniacs. Show him, for example, that
your *Campanula morettiana* has taken root and at
night he will come to steal it from you, murdering and

shooting, for he cannot go on living without it. If he is too much of a coward or too fat to steal it from you, he will cry and implore you to give him the tiniest sprig. Hey, that is what comes of boasting and lording it over him with your treasures.

Or it happens that he finds a little flowerpot at the nursery with no label on it, in which something greenish is coming up. 'And what's this you've got here?' he blurts out to the nurseryman.

'This?' says the horticulturist in bewilderment. 'It's some sort of Bellflower; I'm not sure myself which one it might be.'

'I'll take it,' says the maniac, feigning indifference.

'No,' says the horticulturist. 'I'm not selling this one.'

'Now, look,' the maniac begins touchingly. 'I've been buying from you for such a long time now, so tell me, what harm can it do you? I mean!'

After much discussion, repeatedly going away and coming back again to the intriguing, nameless little pot, making it distinctly clear that he is not going to leave without it, even if he has to hang about here for nine weeks, and so availing himself of all manner of tricks and coercion known to the collector, the rock garden cultivator finally takes the mysterious Bellflower home, chooses the best bed for it in his rockery, plants it with infinite tenderness and every day comes to water it and sprinkle it with all the care which this rarity deserves. And, truly, the Bellflower sprouts like a fountain.

'Look,' the proud owner points out to his guests. 'This is a strange sort of Bellflower, isn't it! No-one has managed to identify it for me yet. I wonder what it'll flower like.'

'That's a Bellflower?' says a guest. 'It's almost got leaves like a Horseradish.'

'A Horseradish, my foot,' the owner objects. 'Why, a Horseradish has got much larger leaves and they're not so shiny. It's definitely a Bellflower. But maybe,' he adds modestly, 'it's a new species.'

Due to the abundant moisture, the said Bellflower grows with astonishing speed. 'Look,' its owner pontificates, 'you said that it's got leaves like a Horseradish. Have you ever seen a Horseradish with such huge leaves? Good Lord, it's some sort of *Campanula gigantea*; it's going to have leaves like plates.'

Well, finally this singular Bellflower starts to put forth a flower stem and on it — well, it is just a

72

Horseradish after all; the devil only knows how it got into the nurseryman's flowerpot!

'Listen,' says the guest after a time, 'where've you put that huge Bellflower? Isn't it flowering anymore?'

'Is it hell! It died on me. You know these tricky rare varieties. I expect it was some sort of hybrid.'

*

It is always a devil getting hold of plants. In March, the nurseryman does not usually despatch your order because it may freeze and the seedlings are not out yet; in April, he does not despatch it either because he has got too many of these orders; and in May, he does not despatch it because mostly everything is already sold out. 'There are no Primroses left; but, if you like, I'll give you a Mullein instead; it's got yellow flowers too.'

But sometimes it does happen that the postman finally brings you a basket of the seedlings which you ordered. Hallelujah! Just here in the border I need something very high to go between the Monk's-hood and the Larkspurs; we'll definitely put a *Dictamnus* there, also called Dittany or the Burning Bush; it's true that the seedling which they've sent is somewhat small, but it will grow like lightning.

A month passes and for some reason the seedling does not want to grow; it looks like a very short blade of grass — if it were not a *Dictamnus* you would say that it were a *Dianthus*. We must water it well to make it grow; and, you see, it has got some sort of pink flowers —

'Look,' the amateur gardener points out to an expert guest. 'It's a very short *Dictamnus*, isn't it?'

'You mean, *Dianthus*,' the guest corrects him.

'Of course, *Dianthus*,' says the host quickly. 'It was a slip of the tongue. It's only that I was just thinking that a *Dictamnus* would do rather better among these high perennials, don't you think?'

*

Every gardening manual will tell you that 'it is best to grow seedlings from seed'. But they do not tell you that, as far as seeds are concerned, nature has its own special customs. It is a law of nature that either not one of the seeds which you have sown will sprout or that they will all sprout indiscriminately. You say to yourself, 'Here some sort of ornamental thistle would do nicely, say a *Cirsium* or an *Onopordum*.' And you buy a packet of both sorts of seed, sowing and

75

rejoicing at the thought of how beautifully the seeds will sprout. After a time, you have to prick them out, and the gardener is pleased to have a hundred and sixty potfuls of wanton seedlings. He says to himself that growing from seed like this is simply the best. And then the seedlings are ready to go into the soil. But what is a person to do with a hundred and sixty thistles? He has already stuck them wherever there was the least inch of soil and he has still got over a hundred and thirty left. To be sure, is he supposed to throw them in the bin when he has brought them up so carefully?

'Dear neighbour, wouldn't you like a *Cirsium* seedling? It's very attractive, you know.'

'Well, all right.'

Praise God, the neighbour has taken thirty seedlings with which he is now running about the garden bemusedly, trying to find somewhere to stick them. Then there is always the neighbour further down and across the road —

God help them when these grow into six-foot ornamental thistles!

BLESSED RAIN

Probably every one of us has some inherited bit of the farmer in him, even if we cannot even grow Geraniums or Sea Onions on the windowsill. Once the sun has shone on us for a week, we begin to look anxiously at the sky and say to one another when we meet, 'It ought to rain.'

'It ought,' says the other townsman. 'I was at Letná the other day and it's already so dry there that the ground is cracking.'

'And I went to Kolín by train the other day,' says the first. 'It seemed terribly dry.'

'We ought to have some proper rain,' sighs the other.

'If it would just rain for at least three days,' adds the first.

But, meanwhile, the sun beats down, Prague gradually begins to smell of the whiff of hot human beings, on the trams human carnality steams gloomily, and people are irritable and rather unsociable.

'I think it's going to rain,' says a sweaty creature.

'It ought to,' groans another.

'If it would just rain for at least a week,' says the

77

first, 'for the grass and that.'

'It's too dry,' states the other.

Meanwhile, the scorching heat of the sun gathers swelteringly, a heavy tension ferments in the air, and storms roll across the sky but relieve neither earth nor man. But once more storms resound on the horizon, the wind blows, saturated with water, and now it is here: cords of rain purl on the pavement, the earth exhales almost audibly, water fizzes, drums, patters, rattles against the windows, raps with thousands of fingers in the gutters, runs in gullies and tinkles in puddles, and you would like to shout with joy, you stick your head out of the window to cool it in the heavenly moisture, you whistle, yell, and would like to stand barefoot in the yellow torrents racing through the streets. Blessed rain, cooling delight of water! Bathe my soul and cleanse my heart, glistening, cold dew. I was wicked with the heat, wicked and lazy; I was lazy and sombre, dull, corporeal and selfish; I was parched with dryness and stifled with heaviness and displeasure. Tinkle, silver kisses, with which the thirsty earth receives the lashing of the drops; hiss, flying veil of water, expiating everything. No miracle of the sun can compare with the miracle of blessed rain. Rush, cloudy water, through the gullies of the earth; water and loosen the thirsty matter which imprisons us. We have all breathed out: the grass, me, the earth, all of us; and now we are fine.

The fizzing downpour has ceased, as though a cord had been pulled; the earth brightens with a silver haze; in a bush a blackbird calls out and fools around like something deranged; and we would like to fool around too, but instead we go out in front of our houses with our heads uncovered, so that we can inhale the fresh, sparkling dampness of the air and of the earth.

'It was a good shower,' we say to one another.

'It was,' we say, 'but it could do with raining a bit more.'

'It could,' we answer, 'but even this was a blessed bit of rain.'

Half an hour later, it rains again, in long, thin, threads. This is that real, silent, good rain; silently and broadly the harvest is raining. It is no longer a splashing, streaming torrent; the airy, peaceful shower whispers softly. Quiet dew, not one drop of yours will be wasted. But the clouds part and the sun leans on the thin threads; the threads snap, the shower disappears, and the earth exhales a warm moisture.

'That was a proper, May rain,' we delight. 'Now it'll green up nicely.'

'A few more drops,' we say, 'and that should do.'

The sun leans full tilt on the earth, a sultry swelter rises from the damp land, breathing heavily and stuffily as in a hotbed. In a corner of the sky a new storm rolls up, you inhale the hot vapour, several heavy drops fall to earth, and from somewhere in another country a wind wafts, drenched with rainy coolness. You tire in the damp air as in a lukewarm bath, you breathe droplets of water, paddle in the streams of water, and see white and grey parcels of vapour gathering in the sky as if the whole world wanted to melt warmly and gently into the May shower.

'It could do with raining a bit more,' we say.

THE GARDENER'S JUNE

June is the main time for hay making, but as far as we urban gardeners go, please do not imagine that one dewy morning we sharpen our scythes and with open-necked shirts and robust swaths mow the sparkling grass until it whistles along, singing folk songs all the while. The whole business is somewhat different. First and foremost, we gardeners want to have English turf, as green as a billiard cloth and as thick as a carpet, perfect turf, an immaculate lawn, sward like velvet, a meadow like a table-top. Well, in early spring we find that this English turf consists of all sorts of bald patches, Dandelions, Clover, clay, Moss and a few, tough, yellowish tufts of grass. First, it must be weeded. At this point, therefore, we squat down and pull all the nasty weeds out of the turf, leaving behind us empty ground, trampled and as bare as if bricklayers had been dancing on it or a herd of zebras. Then, it is watered and left to crack in the sun; whereupon, we decide that it really does need mowing.

On reaching this decision, the inexpert gardener gathers himself and goes to the nearest suburb, where

he finds a well-grazed, bare patch of wasteland with a little, old woman on it and a meagre goat which is gnawing a Hawthorn or a tennis net

'Grandma,' says the gardener affably, 'wouldn't you like some nice grass for your little goat? You can come and cut as much as you like.'

'And what'll you give me for it?' says grandma, after some consideration.

'Five pounds,' says the gardener and returns home to wait for grandma with her goat and sickle. But grandma does not come.

Then the gardener buys himself a sickle and a whetstone and declares that he is not going to ask anyone for any help and that he is going to cut the grass himself. Except that, either the sickle is too blunt or town grass is too tough or something; in short, the sickle will not cut; every stem has to be taken by the tip, stretched out and, with great strength, severed at the base with the sickle, during which the roots usually get torn out too. With sewing scissors it is significantly faster. When the gardener has finally cut, plucked and wrecked his turf as well as possible, he has only a tiny heap of hay raked up to show for his efforts; and he gathers himself and goes to find grandma with the goat again.

'Grandma,' he says cloyingly, 'wouldn't you like a basket of my hay for your goat? It's good, clean hay.'

'And what'll you give me for it?'

'Two pounds,' declares the gardener, and hurries home to wait for grandma to come and fetch the hay. After all, it is a shame to throw away such good hay, isn't it?

In the end, it is the dustman who takes away the hay, but he has to be given a pound. 'Y'know, guv,' he says, 'we're not meant to take it in the cart.'

*

The more expert gardener simply buys a lawn mower. This is a sort of a thing on wheels, it rattles like a machine gun, and when you go over the grass with it, the grass simply flies; I tell you, it is a delight. When a lawn mower comes into a home, all the members of the family, from the grandfather to the grandson, fight over who is going to cut the grass; that is how much fun it is to rattle round and mow luxuriant turf. 'Let go,'

declares the gardener, 'I'll show you how it's done.' Whereupon he moves off across the lawn with the ceremoniousness at once of the engineer and the ploughman.

'It's my turn now,' implores another member of the family.

'Just a bit more,' the gardener sticks to his prerogative and moves off again, rattling and mowing the grass

until it flies about. This is the first, festive haymaking.

'Listen,' the gardener says after a while to another member of the family, 'wouldn't you like to take the mower out and cut the grass? It's very pleasant work.'

'I know,' says the other halfheartedly, 'but I don't really have time today.'

Haymaking, as is well known, is the time for storms. For several days it gathers in the sky and on the earth; the sun is scorching and somewhat unpleasant, the earth cracks and dogs reek; the farmer looks anxiously at the sky and says that it ought to rain. Whereupon, so-called ominous clouds appear and a wild wind breaks out, tearing with it dust, hats and torn-off leaves; then the gardener rushes out into the garden with hair flying, not to defy the elements like a Romantic poet, but to tie back everything that is tossing in the wind, clear away his tools and chairs and

generally resist elemental disaster. As he is trying in vain to tie back the *Delphinium* stems, the first, large, hot drops fall. It grows stifling for a moment, and crack! A heavy downpour splashes to the rumble of thunder. The gardener flees to the verandah and with a heavy heart watches as his little garden tosses about under the buffets of the rain and the gale; and when it is at its worst, he rushes out like a man rescuing a drowning child, to tie back a half-broken Lily. God above, what water! On top of this, hailstones clatter, bounce over the ground, and are swept away in streams of dirty water; and in the gardener's heart anxiety for his garden wrestles with a sort of euphoria which great elemental phenomena arouse in us. Afterwards, it rumbles more sombrely, the torrent turns into a cold rain and thins out into a light shower. The gardener runs into his chilled garden, looks in despair at the lawn clogged with sand, at the broken Irises and decimated flowerbeds and, while the first blackbird is shrieking, calls over the fence to his neighbour, 'Hello, we could still do with a bit more rain. That wasn't enough for the trees.'

The day after, the newspapers write about the calamitous cloud burst which caused awful damage, particularly to the new crops; but they do not write that it caused terrible damage particularly to the Lilies or that it has especially ruined the Oriental Poppies. We gardeners are always overlooked.

*

If it were any use, the gardener would fall on his knees every day and would pray perhaps something like this: 'Lord God, bring it about somehow so that it rains every day from about midnight to three in the morning, but, You know, slowly and warmly enough for it to soak in, but, at the same time, so that it doesn't rain on the Sweet William, Madwort, Rock Rose, Lavender and those other plants which, by Your infinite wisdom, are known to You as drought-loving plants — if You like, I'll write them down for You on a sheet of paper; and let the sun shine all day, but not everywhere (for example, not on the Spiraeas, nor on the Gentians, *Funkia* or *Rhododendrons*) and not too much; let there be lots of dew and only a little wind, plenty of worms, no aphids or slugs, no mildew, and let it rain diluted dung water and pigeon droppings once a week. Amen.' For you should know that is how it was in the Garden of Eden; how else do you suppose that things grew so well there?

*

But just after I said the word 'aphids' I should have added that June is the very month for destroying aphids. There are all sorts of powders, preparations, tinctures, extracts, concoctions and stenches, arsenic, tobacco, soft soap and other poisons for the purpose which the gardener tries one after the other as soon as he discovers that green, plumply soaked aphids are multiplying alarmingly on his Roses. If you use these

products with a certain caution and in right measure, you will find that your Roses sometimes survive this destruction of the aphids without injury, except that it rather singes their leaves and buds. As for the aphids, they thrive during this destruction to an extraordinary extent, so that they cover the Rose sprigs like thick embroidery. Afterwards, it is possible — with loud protestations of disgust — to squash them a sprig at a time. This, then, is how aphids are destroyed; but for a long time afterwards the gardener will reek of tobacco and soft soap.

ON VEGETABLE GROWERS

There are sure to be some people who, reading these edifying reflections, will say indignantly: 'What? This chap here talks about every inedible dwindling but not a word does he say about Carrots, Cucumbers, Kohlrabies or Savoy Cabbages, Cauliflowers or Onions, Leeks or Radishes, why not even about Celery, Chives or Parsley, not to mention a nice head of Cabbage! What sort of gardener is he when, partly out of pride and partly out of ignorance, he ignores the most beautiful things which you can grow, like, for example, this Lettuce patch?'

To this rebuke I would reply that in one of the many chapters of my life I too held sway over several patches of Carrots and Savoy Cabbages and Lettuces and Kohlrabies; I did it, to be sure, out of a sort of romanticism, wanting to indulge in the illusion of being a farmer. In due course, it became clear that I was going to have to munch a hundred and twenty Radishes a day because no-one else in the house would eat them anymore; the following week, I was drowning in Savoy Cabbages, after which came orgies in Kohlrabies, even quite tough ones. There were weeks when I had to chew Lettuce three times a day rather than throw it out. I do not mean to spoil the pleasure of vegetable growers in any way, but what they have grown, so must they eat. If I had to scoff my Roses or nibble at Lily-of-the-valley flowers, I think that I would lose a certain respect for them. Mary, Mary may be quite contrary, but she would have to be really contrary indeed to want to munch her garden.

Besides this, we gardeners already have quite enough enemies: sparrows and blackbirds, children, snails, earwigs and aphids. I ask you, should we open hostilities with caterpillars too? Should we set cabbage white butterflies against us?

Every citizen dreams at some time of what he would do if he were a dictator for a day. In my case, I would order, institute and quash a great many things on that day; among others, I would issue a so-called Raspberry Edict. This would be an order that no gardener, under pain of having his right hand cut off, should plant Raspberries beside a fence. I beseech you, what does a neighbour do to deserve having indestructible Raspberry shoots from his neighbour's garden spring up in the middle of his Rhododendrons? These Raspberries creep yards underground; no fence or wall or trench, why not even barbed wire or a warning sign, will stop them; then a cane sprouts up in the middle of your Carnations or Evening Primroses, and give it a stern talking to! May every one of your Raspberries grow bitter with aphids! May Raspberry sprouts spring up in the middle of your bed! May you grow warts the size of Raspberries! However, if you are ordinary, virtuous gardeners, you will not plant Raspberries beside your fence, nor Knotgrass, nor Sunflowers, nor other plants which will, so to speak, tread on your neighbour's private property.

Now, if you want to please your neighbour, plant Melons beside your fence. Once, a Melon from my neighbour's garden grew on my side of the fence which was so huge, so Canaanite, so record breaking that it inspired the amazement of a whole swathe of columnists, poets, why, even university professors, who could not comprehend how such a gigantic piece of fruit could have squeezed between the palings of the fence. After a time, the said Melon began to look rather wanton and we cut it off and ate it as a punishment.

THE GARDENER'S JULY

According to the canonical law of gardeners, Roses are grafted in July. It is usually done like this: a brier, wilding or stock is prepared on which the grafting needs to be done; also a large amount of bast and, finally, a gardening knife or pruning knife. When everything is ready, the gardener tests the pruning knife's blade on the ball of his thumb; if the pruning knife is sharp enough, it will cut into his thumb and leave a gaping, bloody little opening there. This is later bound in several yards of bandage from which a quite large, full bud emerges on the thumb. This is called grafting Roses. If there is not a brier to hand, it is also possible to bring about this incision into your thumb on other occasions, such as while making stakes, cutting off suckers or withered stalks, trimming bushes, and the like.

*

Having finished this Rose grafting, the gardener finds that he ought to loosen the flattened, solid-baked soil in the flowerbed again. This is done about six times a

94

year and each time the gardener pulls an incredible quantity of stones and other rubbish out of the soil. Evidently, stones are produced by some sort of seeds or eggs or continuously loom out of the mysterious

bowels of the earth; perhaps the earth somehow sweats them. Garden or cultivated soil, also called humus or topsoil, generally consists of particular ingredients which are: clay, manure, rotten leaves, peat, stones, shards from pint bottles, broken bowls, nails, wires, bones, Hussite arrows, foil from chocolate wrappers, bricks, old coins, old smoking pipes, sheet glass, mirrors, old labels, tin pots, bits of string, buttons, shoe soles, dog dirt, coal, pot handles, wash-hand basins, dishcloths, bottles, railway sleepers, milk cans, buckles, horseshoes, tin cans, insulating material, bits of newspaper, and countless other constituents which the astonished gardener wrests from his flowerbeds every time that he hoes. Perhaps one day he will unearth an American stove under his Tulips, Attila's grave or the Sibylline Books; in a cultivated soil everything can be found.

*

But the main July concern, of course, is watering and spraying the garden. If the gardener waters with a watering can, he counts the canfuls like a motorist miles. 'Oof,' he declares with the pride of a record breaker, 'today I have carried forty-five canfuls.' If only you knew what a pleasure it is when cool water trickles and fizzes on parched soil; when it sparkles in the early evening on flowers and leaves overburdened after a keen shower; when the whole garden then exhales moistly and with relief, the way that a thirsty wayfarer does. 'Aaah,' says the wayfarer, wiping the foam from his beard, 'that was the devil of a thirst. Barman, another!' And the gardener runs for another canful for this July thirst.

With a hydrant and a hose it is, of course, possible to water faster and somewhat *en masse*; in a relatively short time we can spray not only the flowerbeds, but the turf, a neighbouring family having tea, pedestrians in the street, the inside of the house, all the members

of our family and, most of all, ourselves. Spraying from a hydrant is amazingly potent, almost like a machine gun; in an instant you can hollow out a crater in the earth, mow down perennials and tear the tops off trees. If you spray the hose against the wind, it will provide you with superb refreshment; it is outright hydropathy when it sprays you right through. A hose, moreover, has a special predilection for developing a hole somewhere in the middle, where you least expect it; and so you stand like a water god in the middle of gushing jets of water, with a long water snake coiled at your feet; it is an overwhelming sight. Then, when you are wet through, you declare with satisfaction that the garden has had enough and you go to dry off. In the meantime, your garden has said 'Oof', has slurped down

your jets of water without even batting an eyelid and is
as dry and thirsty as it was before.

*

German philosophy maintains that crude reality is
simply that which is, whereas the higher moral order
is 'das Sein-Sollende' or that which ought to be. Well,
the gardener, especially in July, profoundly acknowledges this higher order, knowing full well what ought
to be. 'It ought to rain,' the gardener expresses it in his
distinctive way.

It is usually like this: when so-called life-giving sun-
beams bring it above fifty degrees centigrade, when the
grass turns yellow, leaves on plants shrivel and tree

branches droop and wilt with thirst and from the heat, when the earth cracks, bakes solid into stone or crumbles into scorching dust, then as a rule:

1. the gardener's hose punctures, so that he cannot water.

2. something happens at the water board and no water runs at all and you are, as they say, in a pickle — even in a tart and spicy pickle.

At such times, the gardener waters the soil in vain with his own sweat. Just imagine how much he would have to sweat for the needs, let us say, of a smallish lawn. Likewise, it does not help to curse, swear, blaspheme or spit angrily, even if every time that we spit we rush into the garden (every drop of moisture is good!). At this juncture, then, the gardener resorts to that

higher order and starts saying fatalistically, 'It ought to rain.'

'And where are you going for your summer holiday this year?'

'What of it? But it ought to rain.'

'And what do you think about Engliš's resignation?'

'I think it ought to rain.'

Lord, when one thinks of a lovely November rain! For four, five or six days, cool threads of rain fizzle, it is grey and dank, it leaks into your shoes, squelches under your feet and numbs you to the bone.

As I say, it ought to rain.

*

100

Roses and Phloxes, Sneezeweeds and Tickseeds, Daylilies, Gladioli, Bellflowers and Monk's-hoods and Elecampanes and Labrador Teas and Ox-eye Daisies — thank God that there are still enough of these which will flower in these poor conditions. There is always something flowering and something withering; you are forever trimming withered stems, murmuring (to the flower, not to yourself), 'And so now it's over for you too.'

Mind, these flowers really are like women: so beautiful and fresh that you could rest your eyes on them and never absorb all their beauty; something always eludes you. God, that everything which is beautiful is so insatiable! But as soon as they start to wither, then, I do not know, they somehow stop taking trouble over their appearance (I am talking about the flowers), and if one wanted to be rude, one would almost say that they look like sluts. What a shame, my sweet beauty (I am talking about the flowers), what a shame that time passes so; beauty wanes and only the gardener remains.

The gardener's autumn really begins in March; with the first withered Snowdrop.

A BOTANICAL CHAPTER

As is well known, we differentiate glacial flora, steppe flora, Arctic, Pontic, Mediterranean, subtropical, paludal and sundry other types of flora, partly by their origin, and partly by the place in which they are found and thrive.

Well, then, if you are remotely interested in the plant kingdom, you will find that one type of vegetation thrives in coffeehouses and another, let us suppose, at pork butchers' shops, that certain varieties and genera fare particularly well at railway stations and others near signalmen's boxes. Perhaps with detailed, comparative study it could be demonstrated that a different flora prospers on Catholics' windowsills than on the windowsills of unbelievers and progressives, while only artificial flowers really thrive in shopwindows with fancy goods in them, and so on. However, since botanical topography is still, as they say, in its infancy, let us hold to a few sharply delimited and salient botanical groups.

1. Train station flora has two subclasses: platform

vegetation and the stationmaster's garden. On the platform, usually hanging in baskets but sometimes also seen on windowledges or in station windows, Nasturtiums fare particularly well, plus Lobelias, Geraniums, Petunias and Begonias and, at higher-class stations, sometimes also Dracaenas. Train station flora is characterised by its unusually profuse and colourful bloom. The stationmaster's garden is botanically less distinctive; Roses can be found in it, Forget-me-nots, Pansies, Lobelias, Honeysuckle and other sociologically less differentiated species.

2. Railway flora grows in signalmen's gardens. It includes, in particular, Marsh Mallow, which is also known as Hollyhock, and Sunflowers, as well as *Tropaeolum*, rambling Roses, Dahlias and sometimes also Asters; obviously, these are mostly plants which stick out over the fence, perhaps to please the passing engine driver. Wild railway flora grows on railway embankments; in particular, it consists of Rock Roses, Snapdragons, Mulleins, Corn Camomile, Viper's-bugloss, Thyme and several other railway species.

3. Butcher's flora grows in butchers' shopwindows, among the chopped loins, joints, lamb and salamis. It includes a rather small number of species, in particular *Aucuba* and *Asparagus sprengeri* and, among Cacti, *Cereus* and *Echinopsis*; in pork butchers' shops, *Araucaria* can also be found in flowerpots, and sometimes Primroses too.

103

4. Pub flora includes two Oleanders at the entrance and Aspidistras in the windows. Pubs which go in for so-called 'specials' usually have *Cineraria* in the windows too. In restaurants they also grow Dracaenas, Philodendrons, Broad-leaved Begonias, variegated Coleuses, Lantanas, Ficuses and generally any plants which erstwhile society reporters used to describe in such fitting terms as 'the show was bathed in the luxuriant verdure of tropical vegetation'. In coffeehouses, only Aspidistras do well; but then on coffeehouse terraces, Lobelias, Petunias, Spiderworts and even Laurel and Ivy grow in abundance.

As far as I am aware, no plants do well in bakers' shops, gunsmiths', car showrooms, farm machinery outlets, ironmongers', furriers', stationers', hat makers' and many other businesses. Office windows have either nothing in them at all or red and white Geraniums. Office plants depend on the will and good favour of either the office caretaker or the office manager. Besides, a certain tradition prevails here; while diverse vegetation thrives in the sphere of railways, at post offices and telegraph offices nothing grows at all; private offices are, from a botanical point of view, more productive than government offices, among which the Inland Revenue's offices in particular are a downright desert.

In a botanical class of its own, of course, is cemetery flora, and then, needless to say, the ceremonial flora which enwraps the plaster busts of honoured people; this includes Oleanders, Laurels, Palms and, at worst, Aspidistras.

As for window flora, there are two sorts: the poor and the rich. The flora at the homes of poorer people is usually better; besides that of the rich usually perishes while they are on their summer holiday.

Of course, this is far from exhausting the botanical abundance of the various places where plants occur. Some time, I should like to ascertain what type of people grow Fuchsias and what Passion Flowers, what occupation Cactus growers have, and so on. Perhaps there is a particular Communist flora or Popular Party flora, or perhaps one will catch on. Great are the treasures of the world; every trade, why even every political party, could have its own flora.

THE GARDENER'S AUGUST

August is usually the time when the domestic gardener forsakes his garden of wonders and goes on
holiday. Throughout the year, admittedly, he has
emphatically declared that this year he would not be
going anywhere, that a little garden like his was better
than any holiday resort, and that he, a gardener, was

not such a fool and nincompoop as to trudge somewhere on a train and all that damned nonsense;
nevertheless, when the summer comes, he too flees the
town, either because the migratory instinct has burst
out in him or to keep up appearances in front of the
neighbours. Of course, he departs with a heavy heart,
full of fear and anxiety for his garden; and he does not
leave until he has found a friend or relation to whom
he can entrust his garden for the duration.

'Look,' he says, 'there's no work to be done in the
garden at the moment anyway; it's enough if you just
look in once every three days and if, by chance, something or other isn't right, send me a card and I'll come.
Well, I'm relying on you. As I say, five minutes will be
enough, just to pop your head in.'

After which, he departs, thus laying his garden on
the heart of his obliging fellow being. The next day, this
fellow being receives a letter: 'I forgot to tell you that the
garden needs watering every day, preferably at five in
the morning or at about seven in the evening. There's
nothing to it, just screw the hose onto the hydrant and
water for an hour. You will need to water the conifers
all over, please, and thoroughly, and the lawn too. If you
see a weed anywhere, pull it out. That's all.'

A day later: 'It's terribly dry. Please give every
Rhododendron about two canfuls of lukewarm water,
every conifer five canfuls and the other trees about
four. Any perennials which are flowering at the
moment need a lot of water; write by return to let me
know what's flowering. The dead stems want cutting

107

off. It would be good if you could loosen all the flowerbeds with a hoe, then the soil will breathe better. If there are any aphids on the Roses, buy some tobacco extract and spray the Roses with it when it's dewy or after it's rained. There's nothing else that needs doing at the moment.'

On the third day: 'I forgot to tell you that the lawn needs mowing; you'll be able to do it without any bother with the mower, and what the mower doesn't take off you can cut with the shears. But please be aware! After it's been mown, the grass needs raking well and then sweeping with a broom. Otherwise, the lawn will get bald patches. And remember to water; give it lots of water!'

On the fourth day: 'If a storm gets up, please do run and have a look at my garden; a heavy downpour sometimes causes damage and it's good to be right on the spot. If mildew appears on the Roses, sprinkle them with flowers of sulphur early in the morning, while it's still dewy. Tie the tall perennials back to their stakes so that the wind won't break them. It's glorious here, the Mushrooms are growing, and the swimming's great. Don't forget to water the *Ampelopsis* next to the house every day; it's dry there. Save some Icelandic Poppy seeds in a packet for me. I hope you've mown the lawns by now. Otherwise, there's nothing else, except to kill the earwigs.'

On the fifth day: 'I'm sending you a little box of flowers which I have dug up here in the woods. There are

various Orchids, wild Lilies, Pasque Flowers, Pyrolas, Lungworts, Anemones and other plants. The minute you get the box, open it, water the seedlings and plant them somewhere in the garden in the shade. Put some peat and leafmould on them. Plant them straightaway and water them three times a day!! Please cut off the suckers on the Roses!!'

On the sixth day: 'I'm sending you a basket of wild flowers by express. Put them straight into the ground. At night, you need to go into the garden with a torch and kill the snails. It would be good if you could weed the paths. I hope watching over my garden isn't taking too much of your time and that you're enjoying some pleasant moments in it.'

Meanwhile, the obliging fellow being, conscious of his responsibilities, waters, mows, hoes, weeds and wanders about with the posted seedlings, searching for where in the devil's name to plant them; he is sweaty and splattered from head to foot; with horror, he notices that a dwindling is withering here, and some stems have broken there, and the lawn has developed ergot here, and that the whole garden looks somehow rather parched, and he curses the moment that he took this burden on himself, and prays for autumn to come.

And, in the meantime, the garden's owner thinks with unease of his little flowers and lawns, sleeps badly, curses because the obliging fellow being is not writing him a report every day on the state of the garden, and counts the days to his return, every other day

110

sending a box of wild flowers and a letter with a dozen urgent instructions. Finally, he does return. With his suitcases still in his hands he rushes into the garden and looks round with moist eyes —

'The loafer, the clot, the swine!' he thinks to himself bitterly. 'He has ruined my garden!'

'Thank you,' he says dryly to his fellow being and, as a vivid reproach, seizes the hose to water the neglected garden. (The idiot! he thinks in the depth of his soul. To entrust something to him! As long as I live, I shall never be such a fool and nincompoop again as to go away for the summer!)

*

Oh, wild flowers — one way or another the garden fanatic digs these out of the soil to incorporate them into his garden. It is even worse with other natural objects. 'Damn,' thinks the gardener, looking at the Matterhorn or at Gerlachovka. 'If I had this mountain like that in my garden, and this piece of virgin forest with its forest giants, and this glade, and this mountain torrent, or, better still, this lake. This silken meadow would do nicely in the garden too, as well as a bit of seashore, and the ruin of a Gothic monastery wouldn't go amiss either. And I'd like to have that thousand-year-old lime, and that ancient fountain would look pretty good in my garden, and what about a herd of stags or the odd chamois, or at least this avenue of age-old Poplars, that rock over there, this

river, that Oak grove, or this nice, white and blue waterfall, or at least this quiet, green valley'.

If it were possible to do a deal with the devil somehow so that he would fulfil the gardener's every wish, the gardener would sell him his soul; but, mind you, the poor devil would pay damnably dear for this soul. 'Rotten chap,' he would say at last. 'Rather than making me toil like this, beat it off to heaven instead — you don't belong anywhere else anyway'. And, lashing his tail peevishly until he knocked off some Feverfew and Sneezeweed flowers with it, he would go on his way and leave the gardener to his immodest, insatiable desires.

*

You should know that I am talking about the garden gardener and not about fruit growers and vegetable growers. May the fruit grower beam over his Apples and Pears, may the vegetable grower rejoice at his larger-than-life Kohlrabies, Pumpkins and Celery. The true gardener feels in all his bones that August is already a sort of turning-point. Whatever is flowering is already hastily looking to wither; now the time of Michaelmas Daisies and Chrysanthemums is coming again, and then good night! But, but, there's still you, radiant Phlox, vicarage flower, and you, Golden Groundsel and Goldenrod, golden Cone Flower, golden *Harpalium*, golden Sunflower, there's still you and me, we won't give in yet, far from it! Spring lasts the whole year and youth lasts the whole of life; there is always something to flower. We only say that it is autumn; in reality, we are coming into bloom with another sort of flower, we are growing underground, we are putting on new shoots, and there is always something to do. Only those who have their hands in their pockets say that it is changing for the worse; but whoever flowers and bears fruit, even if it is in November, knows nothing of autumn but only of golden summer and knows nothing of decay but only of germination. Michaelmas Daisy, dear chap, the year is so long that it does not even have an end.

ON CACTUS GROWERS

If I call them sectarians, it is not because they grow
Cacti with great zeal; this actual state might be called
passion, eccentricity or mania. The essence of sectari-
anism is not that something is done zealously, but that
something is believed in zealously. There are Cactus
growers who believe in powdered marble, whereas others
believe in brick dust, and others still in charcoal; some
praise watering, while others condemn it. There are
some profound mysteries of the True Cactus Soil which
no Cactus lover will divulge to you, even if you were to
break him on the wheel. All these sects, observances,
rites, schools and lodges, as well as the wild and hermit
Cactus lovers, will swear to you that only by dint of their
Method have they achieved such miraculous results.
Look at this *Echinocactus myriostigma*. Have you ever
seen anyone else with an *Echinocactus myriostigma*
like it? Well, I'll tell you, so long as you don't tell anyone
else: you mustn't water it, but just sprinkle it. There. —
What! exclaims another Cactus lover. Who ever heard
that *Echinocactus myriostigma* should be sprinkled?
Do you want the top to catch cold? Oh ho, sir, if you

don't want your *Echinocactus* to die straightaway of rot you should just wet it by putting it in its flowerpot once a week in soft water at a temperature of 23.789 degrees Celsius. Then it'll grow like a beanstalk. — Jesus Christ, shouts a third Cactus lover, look at the murderer! If you soak the flowerpot, sir, it'll get covered in green algae, the soil will go acid and you'll be up the creek, yes you will, up the creek; plus, your *Echinocactus myriostigma*'s roots will go rotten. If you don't want the soil to go acid you must water it every other day with sterilised water and then in just such a way that 0.111111 grammes of water falls on every cubic centimetre of soil at exactly half a degree warmer than the air. — At which, all three Cactus lovers begin shouting at once and setting to each other with fists, teeth, hooves and claws; but, as is the way of the world, the real truth will not be revealed by even these methods.

*

The truth is, of course, that Cacti deserve this peculiar passion, precisely because they are mysterious. A Rose is beautiful but it is not mysterious; among mysterious plants are the Lily, Gentian, Golden Fern, Tree of Knowledge, ancient trees generally, some Mushrooms, the Mandrake, the Orchid, glacial flowers, poisonous and medicinal herbs, Water Lilies, Mesembryanthemums and Cacti. What the mystery resides in, I will not tell you. Mystery simply has to be acknowledged so that we can find it and pay homage to it. So, there are

Cacti which look like sea urchins, Cucumbers and Marrows, candlesticks, jugs, a priest's biretta and a snakes' nest, which are covered in scales, teats, manes, claws, warts, bayonets, yataghans and stars, which are plump and lanky, bristly like a regiment of lancers, sharp like a column brandishing sabres, rounded, woody and wrinkled, marked with rashes, bearded, surly, morose, spiky like a kerf, woven like a basket, and similar to tumours, animals and weapons: the most masculine of all the seed-bearing plants of their type which were created on the third day. ('It beats me,' said the Creator, himself surprised at what he had created.) You can love them without touching them improperly, kissing them or pressing them to your breast; they do not care for any intimacy or other such frivolity; they are as hard as rock, armed to the teeth, and determined to stand their ground. Get lost, paleface, or I'll shoot! A small assortment of Cacti like this looks like an encampment of warlike goblins. Cut off this warrior's head or hand and a new, armed figure will grow out of it, brandishing swords and daggers. Life is a battle.

But there are mysterious moments when this defiant, irritable tough somehow forgets himself and loses himself in daydreams; then a flower bursts out of him, a big, brilliant flower, a priestly flower among upraised weapons. It is a great favour and a precious event which does not happen to everyone in a hurry. I tell you, maternal pride is nothing next to the swaggering and boasting of the Cactus grower whose Cactus has flowered.

117

THE GARDENER'S SEPTEMBER

In its way, from a gardening point of view, September is a rewarding and excellent month; not only because Goldenrods, Michaelmas Daisies and Indian Chrysanthemums flower at this time and not only because of you, heavy and astonishing Dahlias. You should know, you unbelievers, that September is the chosen month for everything which flowers a second time, the month of the second bloom, month of the ripening vine. All of these are the mysterious virtues of the month of September, full of deep intent; on top of all of which, it is the month when the earth opens up once more so that we can plant again! Those things should now go into the ground which need to establish themselves by the spring; which gives us gardeners the opportunity to run about at nurseries again, have a look at their seedlings, and choose some treasures for the coming spring, and, moreover, for me to have the opportunity to stop on the cycle of the year at just the point of these experts and pay them my own tribute.

The great gardener or nurseryman is usually a tee-totaller, a non-smoker and, in a word, a virtuous man;

in history, he is known neither for outstanding crimes
nor for martial or political deeds; his name is usually
immortalised in some new Rose or *Dahlia* or Apple;
this glory — usually anonymous or hidden behind
another name — is enough for him. By some peculiar
freak of nature, he is usually a stout, outright hulking
person, perhaps so that a suitable contrast can there-
by be created with the slight, filigree gracefulness of
flowers; or nature adapted him in the image of Cybele,

to demonstrate his generous paternity. Truly, if such a nurseryman prods a finger into his flowerpots, it is almost as if he were giving the breast to his young wards. He despises garden designers, who in turn regard nurserymen as vegetable growers. You know, they do not consider cultivating nature to be a trade but a science and an art; it is outright crushing when they say of a competitor that he is a good tradesman.

One does not go to a nurseryman as to a trader in collars or ironware, to say what you want to buy, to pay, and go on your way again. One goes to a nurseryman to have a chat, to ask what this is called, and to inform him that that *Hutchinsia* which you bought from him last year is doing well, to lament that the *Mertensia* suffered this year, and to beg him to show you what is new. One should argue with him about whether 'Rudolf Goethe' or 'Emma Bedau' is better (they are Asters), as well as quarrel about whether Trumpet Gentian prefers loam or peat.

After these and many other conversations, you choose a new Madwort (blast, but where am I going to put it?), a Valerian which the blight robbed you of, and a little pot which you cannot agree with the nurseryman about as to what is actually in it; and, having thus spent several hours in instructive, noble conversation, you pay the man, who is not a tradesman, about five or six quid, and that is it. And yet the true nurseryman prefers to see you, tormentor, than the bigwig who arrives in his stinking car and sets him to selecting sixty types of 'your best flowers — but they must be first rate'.

Every nurseryman solemnly swears that he has absolutely wretched soil in his garden, that he does not manure, water or even cover up for the winter. Evidently, he is implying by this that his flowers grow so well out of sheer affection for him. There is something in this. In gardening, a person must have a lucky hand or some sort of higher grace. The true gardener

121

need only jab a piece of leaf into the ground and any sort of plant will grow from it, while we laymen lovingly rear from seedlings, water them, breathe on them, feed them horn powder or baby powder and in the end they somehow dry up on us and wither. I think that there is some sort of magic in it, much like in hunting and in medicine.

*

It is the secret dream of every passionate gardener to produce a new species. My God, if I could get a yellow Forget-me-not to grow, or a Forget-me-not-blue Poppy, or a white Gentian. What, is a blue one more beautiful? It does not matter; but there has never yet been a white Gentian. And then, you know, even on the subject of flowers one is a bit of a chauvinist; if a Czech Rose were to win in the whole world over some American 'Independence Day' or French 'Herriot' we would swell with pride and burst with joy.

*

I sincerely advise you: if you have got a bit of a slope or terrace in your garden, make a rockery. In the first place, a rockery is very beautiful when pillows of Saxifrage, Aubrietia, Madwort, Rockcress and other gorgeous, alpine plants are growing; in the second, simply building a rockery is a remarkable and engrossing business. A man who is building a rockery feels

122

like a Cyclops when, so to speak, he piles boulder upon boulder with elemental strength, builds hills and valleys, moves mountains and marks out rocky cliffs. When, broken-backed, he has then completed his gigantic work, he finds that it looks somewhat different from the romantic mountain range which he had envisaged, that his creation resembles a small pile of

rocks and stones. Do not worry; in a year these stones will turn into the most beautiful flowerbed, sparkling with tiny flowers and overgrown with the prettiest pillows; and your delight will be great. I tell you, build a rockery.

*

There is no denying it any longer: it is autumn. You recognise it by the fact that Michaelmas Daisies and autumn Chrysanthemums are flowering — these autumn flowers bloom with exceptional vigour and abundance; they do not make much of a fuss, and one flower looks much like another, but what a lot of them there are! I tell you, this flowering at a mature age is mightier and more passionate than those restless, fleeting tricks of the young spring. There is the reason and consistency of the adult man in it: if you are going to flower, do it properly; and have lots of honey so that the bees will come. What is a falling leaf next to this rich, autumnal blooming? What, do you not see that there is no tiring?

SOIL

When, in her young days, my late mother used to read
her fortune from the cards, she would always whisper
over one pile, 'What am I treading on?' At the time, I
could not understand why she was so interested in
what she was treading on. Only after very many years
has it begun to interest me too. I have discovered, to
wit, that I am treading on the earth.

We do not really care what we are treading on; we
rush somewhere like mad people and at most glimpse
what beautiful clouds there are up here or what a
beautiful horizon there is back there or what beautiful
blue mountains; but we do not look beneath our feet
to be able to say and celebrate that the soil is beautiful
here. You should have a garden the size of a postage
stamp; you should have at least one small flowerbed to
learn what you are treading on. Then you would see,
dear boy, that not even clouds are as varied, beautiful
and dreadful as the soil beneath your feet. You would
be able to recognise soil which is acid, viscid, clayey,
cold, stony and nasty; you would be able to distinguish
topsoil as airy as gingerbread, as warm, light and good

126

as bread, and you would say that it was beautiful, as you now say about women or clouds. You would feel a particular, sensual pleasure as you drove your stick a yard into the crumbly, friable soil or as you crushed a clod in your fist to sample its airy, moist warmth.

And if you cannot appreciate this singular beauty, then may fate bestow a few square yards of clay upon you as a punishment, clay like tin, substantial, primeval clay, from which a coldness oozes, which will warp under your spade like chewing gum, bake solid in the sun and turn acid in the shade; a clay which is maleficent, unyielding, greasy and kiln-ready, as slippery as a snake and as dry as brick, as airtight as sheet metal and as heavy as lead. And now break it up with a pick, chop it with a spade, smash it with a hammer, turn it over and cultivate it, cursing loudly and lamenting. Then you will understand what enmity is and the obduracy of inanimate, sterile matter which ever did refuse to become a soil of life and still does now; and you will appreciate what a frightful struggle life must have engaged in, inch by inch, to take hold on the soil of the earth, whether that life be called vegetation or man.

And then you will also recognise that you have to give more to the soil than you take from it; you have to break it up and feed it with lime, and heat it with warm manure, sprinkle ashes on it lightly, and flood it with air and sunshine. Then the baked clay begins to fall apart and crumble as if it were breathing quietly; it yields loosely under your spade and with conspicuous

127

willingness; it is warm and pliant in your palm; it is tamed. I tell you, to tame a few yards of soil is a great victory. Now it lies here, active, loose and warm. You would like to crumble all of it and rub it between your fingers to assure yourself of your victory. You do not even think about what you are going to sow in it now. What, is the sight of this dark, airy soil not beautiful enough? Is it not more beautiful than a bed of Pansies or a Carrot patch? You almost envy the vegetation which is going to take possession of this noble, human achievement called topsoil.

And from this time on you will not walk over the earth again not knowing what you are treading on. You will test every pile of earth and every bit of field in your palm and with your stick in the same way that another person might look at the stars, at people or at Violets; you will go into raptures over black topsoil, lovingly rub silky, forest leafmould, balance compact turf in your hand and weigh featherlight peat. 'Good Lord!' you will say, 'I'd like a truckful of this; and, damn it, a wagonful of this leafmould would do me some good; and this humus here, to sprinkle on top, and a couple of these cowpats here, and a pinch of this river sand, and a few barrowfuls of this rotten wood pulp, and a bit of this mud from the stream here, and these scrapings from the road wouldn't be bad, eh? And also the odd bit of phosphate and horn filings, but, heavens, this lovely, arable soil would do me too!' There are soils which are as fat as bacon, as light as a feather, as loose as cake, fair and black, dry and plumply soaked, which are all

128

very varied and noble kinds of beauty; whereas ugly and contemptible is everything which is greasy, cloddish, wet, solid, cold, sterile and given to man to make him curse unredeemed matter; which is all just as ugly as the coldness, obduracy and malice of human souls.

THE GARDENER'S OCTOBER

We say that it is October; we say that nature is going to sleep. The gardener knows better and will tell you that October is as good a month as April. You should know that October is the first month of spring, a month of underground budding and sprouting, of hidden flowering and burgeoning buds. Just poke a little into the soil and you will find ready-formed shoots as thick as your thumb and fragile sprouts and eager roots — it is no use, spring is here; go out, gardener, and plant (just be careful not to cut a budding *Narcissus* bulb in two with your spade).

So, of all the months, October is the month for planting and transplanting. In early spring, the gardener stands over his flowerbed, from which the odd bud tip is beginning to peep out here and there, and says to himself contemplatively, 'It's a tad bare and empty here. I'm going to have to plant something more.' After a few months, the gardener stands over this flowerbed, in which in the meantime six-foot *Delphinium* spikes have sprung up, a jungle of Feverfews, a forest of Bellflowers and the devil knows

130

what else, and says to himself contemplatively, 'It's a tad overgrown and dense here. I'm going to have to pull something up, thin it, and plant it out.' In October, the gardener stands over this flowerbed, from which a dry leaf or bare stem is sticking out here and there, and says to himself contemplatively, 'It's a tad bare and empty here. I'll plant something more, like six Phloxes or the odd large *Aster.*' And he goes and does just this. The gardener's life is full of change and the active will.

Murmuring with mysterious satisfaction, the gardener in October finds bare patches in his garden. 'Hell's bells', he says to himself, 'I suppose something must have died on me here. Let's see, I'm going to have to plant something in this empty space, maybe a Goldenrod or, better still, a Bugbane; I haven't got one of those yet; but an *Astilbe* would get on best here; although for the autumn a *Pyrethrum uliginosum*

would go well; but then a Leopard's Bane wouldn't be bad for the spring either. Wait, I'll put a Bergamot here — either a 'Sunset' or a 'Cambridge Scarlet'; a Daylily would do well here without any trouble too.' After which, he heads off home in deep contemplation, remembering on the way that a Whorlflower is a rewarding plant too, not to mention a Tickseed, but even a *Betonica* should not be sneezed at. Then he hurriedly orders a Goldenrod from some garden outfit, a Bugbane, an *Astilbe*, a *Pyrethrum uliginosum*, a Leopard's Bane, a Bergamot, a Daylily, a Whorlflower, a Tickseed and a *Betonica*, and on top of these adds an *Anchusa* and a Sage, then rages for several days when the plants do not come and do not come; then the postman brings him a great basket of them, whereupon he rushes to the bare patch with a spade. With the first dig, he prizes up a clump of roots on which a whole cluster of buds is thronged. 'Damn,' groans the gardener, 'why, I've got a Globeflower planted here!'

*

Yes, there are fanatics who want everything in their garden belonging to the sixty-eight genera of dicotyledonous plants, the fifteen genera of monocotyledons, the two genera of gymnosperms — of the cryptograms, at least all the ferns, because Club Mosses and Mosses are a nightmare. On the other hand, there are even more fanatical fanatics who dedicate their lives to a single species, but they want and must have this species in every hitherto cultivated and named variety. So, for instance, there are bulb growers dedicated to the worship of Tulips, Hyacinths, Lilies, Glory-of-the-snows, Daffodils, Bunch-flowered Narcissi and other bulbous wonders; plus *Primula* growers and *Auricula* growers who pay exclusive homage to Primroses, as well as *Anemone* growers initiated into the order of windflowers; plus *Iris* growers or 'Irisites' who would

134

die of grief if they did not have everything belonging to the Apogon, Pogoniris, Regelia, Oncocyclus, Juno and Xiphium subgenera, not including the hybrids. There are Delphiniumites growing Larkspurs; there are Rose growers or 'Rosarians' who only associate with Frau Druschki, Mme. Herriot, Mme. Caroline Testout, Herr Wilhelm Kordes, M. Pernet and numerous other personalities who have been reincarnated as Roses; there are fanatical Phloxists or Philofloxosophers who, when their Phloxes bloom in August, loudly scorn Chrysanthemumites, who return the favour in October when *Chrysanthemum indicum* is in bloom; there are melancholy *Aster* growers who, of all the pleasures of life, give preference to Michaelmas Daisies; but of all the fanatics, the wildest (with the exception, of course, of Cactus growers) are *Dahlia* growers or 'Georgians'[†], who will pay a staggering amount for some new American *Dahlia*, even as much as five pounds. Of all of these, only bulb growers have any sort of historical tradition; why, they even have their own patron saint, namely, St. Joseph, who, as is well known, has a Madonna Lily in his hand, although these days he would be able to procure himself of a *Lilium brownii leucanthum*, which is even whiter. Then again, no saint appears with a Phlox or a *Dahlia*; as a result, there are people dedicated to the worship of these plants who are sectarians and who sometimes even establish their own churches.

[†]*Georgians*: This is a pun on the Czech word for Dahlia, 'jiřina.' 'Jiřina' also means 'Georgina' and 'Georgiana.'

Why should these cults not have their own *Lives of the Saints*? Just imagine, say, the life of St. Georginus of Dahlia. Georginus was a virtuous and pious gardener who, after lengthy prayers, succeeded in cultivating the first Dahlias. When the pagan emperor Phloxinian heard about this he flared with anger and sent his bailiffs to arrest the pious Georginus. 'You cabbage grower!' roared Emperor Phloxinian. 'Now you will bow down to these faded Phloxes!' 'I will not,' answered

136

Georginus steadfastly, 'because Dahlias are Dahlias, but a Phlox is just a Phlox.' 'Cut him to pieces!' yelled the cruel Phloxinian; and they cut St. Georginus of Dahlia to pieces and laid waste to his garden and sprinkled green vitriol and sulphur on it; but out of the dismembered pieces of St. Georginus's body were formed the bulbs of all future Dahlias, namely, Peony-flowered Dahlias, *Anemone*-flowered, Single-flowered and Cactus-flowered Dahlias, Star Dahlias, Ball Dahlias, Pompons, Lilliputs, Rosettes, Collerettes and the hybrid Dahlias.

*

An autumn like this is a very fertile time; by comparison, spring is, if I may say so, a tad measly. Autumn likes to work on a grand scale. Do you ever get a spring Violet growing ten feet high or a Tulip growing and growing until it outgrows your trees? There you are, then; and yet you can plant a Michaelmas Daisy or two in early spring and by October a six-foot, virgin forest will have grown from them which you do not dare step into for fear of not being able to find your way out again; or you put a Sneezeweed- or Sunflower-root in the soil in April and now golden flowers nod rather ironically at you from on high, where you cannot reach them, not even if you stand on tiptoe. From time to time the gardener does find that things get a bit out of hand. So, in autumn transplanting of flowers is carried out. Every year the gardener carries his little perennials round like a cat her kittens; and every year

he says to himself with satisfaction, 'There! Now I've got everything planted and in order.' The following year he will sigh again with the same satisfaction. A garden is never finished. In this respect, a garden is like the human world and all human undertakings.

ON THE BEAUTIES OF
AUTUMN

I could write about the blazing colours of autumn, about wistful mists, the souls of the dead, and phenomena in the sky, about the last Asters and the little, red Rose which is still trying to bloom, or about will-o'-the-wisps in the twilight, the smell of cemetery candles, dry leaves and other whimsical things. But I would like to give testimony and praise to another beauty of our Czech autumn: Sugar Beet.

No other harvest of the land exists on such a grand scale as Sugar Beet. Grain is gathered in barns and Potatoes in cellars, but Sugar Beet is gathered in mounds, it accumulates into hillocks and grows into Sugar Beet hill ranges next to rural railway stations. Cart after cart takes away the white heads in an endless procession; from morning to night men with shovels stack the heaps higher and higher and arrange them neatly in geometrical pyramids. Every other fruit of the earth is somehow dispersed along every tiny path into every human habitation. Sugar Beet gushes in a single stream: to the nearest train-line or the nearest sugar refinery. It is a harvest on a large scale; it is a parade *en masse*; it is like a military display. They are brigades, divisions and army corps which line up for transportation. Hence they are arranged in military order; geometry is the beauty of the mass. Beet growers build their storage pits like monumental, angular constructions; it almost becomes a form of architecture. A heap of Potatoes cannot be called a construction; but a heap of Sugar Beet is no pile, it is a building. Townspeople do not particularly like Sugar Beet country; however, now, in autumn, it acquires a certain grandeur. An orderly pyramid of Sugar Beet has something captivating about it. It is a monument to the fruitful earth.

*

But let me drink to the most slighted beauty of the autumn. I know that you have not got a field and you do not gather Sugar Beet in great heaps, but have you ever manured your garden? When they bring a chap a full cartload of it and tip out the warm, smoking heap, you walk round it, weigh it with your eyes and nose and say appreciatively, 'God bless, this is good manure.'

'Good,' you say, 'but a tad light.'

'Nothing but straw,' you think, discontentedly. 'There's hardly any dung in it.'

Away with you, you who hold your noses, taking a wide berth round this noble, fresh heap; you do not know what good manure is. And when the flowerbeds

get what belongs to them, you have a slightly mystical
sense of having done the earth some good.

*

Bare trees are not such a forlorn sight; they look a bit
like brooms or besoms and a bit like scaffolding ready
for building. But if there is a last leaf on one of these
bare trees, quivering in the wind, it is like the last flag
flying on a battlefield, like a standard which a dead
man's hand is clutching on the field of the slain. We
fell, but we did not surrender; our colours are still
flying.

*

And the Chrysanthemums have not given in yet. They
are fragile and airy, merely sketched in white or pink
foam, frozen stiff like young ladies in ball gowns. Is
there too little sunlight? Are grey fogs oppressing us?
Are dank rains dragging over us? No matter. The main
thing is to flower. It is only people who moan about
poor conditions; Chrysanthemums do not.

Even the gods have their seasons. In summer one
may be a pantheist, one may think of oneself as a
part of nature; but in autumn a person can think of
himself only as a person. Even if we do not mark our
foreheads with the sign of the Cross, we all slowly
return to the birth of man. Every home fire burns in
honour of the household gods. Love of home is the
same ritual as worship of a celestial deity.

THE GARDENER'S NOVEMBER

I know that there are many fine jobs, such as writing for the newspapers, voting in parliament, sitting on a board of directors, or signing official bumf; but however nice and praiseworthy they all are, a person doing them does not cut the same figure or have such a monumental, plastic and outright sculptural bearing as a man with a spade. Friend, when you stand in your flowerbed like that, resting with one foot on your spade, wiping away the sweat and saying 'Oof', you look just like an allegorical sculpture. It would be fitting if you were to be carefully dug up, lifted, roots and all, and placed on a plinth with the inscription, 'The Triumph of Work', or, 'Lord of the Earth', or some such. I say this because now is exactly the time for it: that is, for digging.

Yes, in November the soil should be turned over and loosened. To scoop up a spadeful of it is as delicious and epicurean a sensation as if you were scooping up a ladleful or spoonful of food. Good soil, like good food, should be neither too greasy, nor heavy, nor cold, nor very wet, nor very dry, nor sticky, nor hard, nor

HOMO
HORT. EDULIS

crumbly, nor raw; it should be like bread, like gingerbread, like a sweet bun, like leavened dough; it should
separate, but not crumble; it should break under your
spade, but not clack; it should not form benches or

heads or honeycombs or dumplings, but when you turn over a spadeful, it should sigh with pleasure and fall apart in clods and bitty topsoil. This, then, is a tasty, edible soil, cultured and noble, a deep, moist soil, permeable, breathing and soft, in short, a good soil, just as there are good people; and, as is well known, in this vale of tears there is nothing better.

You should know, garden man, that in these autumn days you can still transplant. First, a bush or

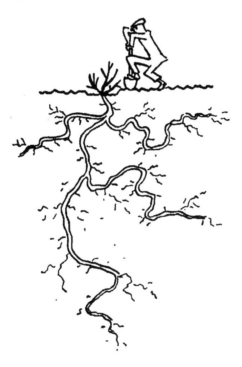

a tree is hoed and dug round as deeply as possible.
Then, it is caught hold of from underneath with a
spade, at which point the spade usually breaks in two.
There are some people, mainly critics and public
speakers, who like to speak of roots; for example, they
declare that we should return to our roots, or that
some evil should be uprooted, or that we should pen-
etrate to the root of something. Well, I should like to
see them if they had to dig out (with the corresponding
roots), let us say, a three-year-old Quince. I would gladly be witness to Mr. Arne Novák plunging down to the
roots of perhaps only so small a bush as a Butcher's
Broom. I would like to watch Mr. Zdeněk Nejedlý
uprooting, let us suppose, an old Poplar. I think that
after some pains they would straighten their backs and
utter only a single word. I bet my bottom dollar that
this word would be 'Damn!' I tried it with some
Cydonias and I can verify that working with roots is
hard and that it is better to leave roots where they are.
They know full well why they want to be so deep. I
would guess that they do not care for our attention. It
is better to let roots be and to improve the soil instead.

*

Yes, to improve the soil. A cartload of manure is at its
most beautiful when it is delivered on a frosty day, so
that it is smoking like a sacrificial pyre. When its
vapour rises up to the heavens, He who understands
all sniffs on high and says, 'Ah, that's some fine

145

manure!' At this point, of course, we have the opportunity to speak of the mysterious cycle of life; a horse eats Oats and then dispatches them on to the Carnations or Roses which, because of this, will praise God the following year with a scent so lovely that it defies description. Well, the gardener can already discern this lovely scent in the smoking, strawy pile of dung, and he sniffs appreciatively and strews this gift of God carefully over the whole garden, just as if he

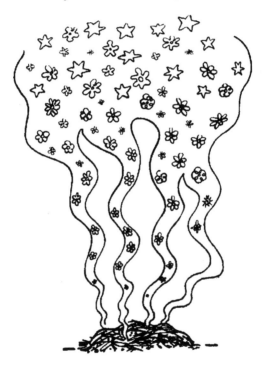

were spreading marmalade on his child's slice of bread. Here you are, little podge, I hope you enjoy it! Mme. Herriot, I'll give you a whole pile because you flowered so bronze and prettily; so that you won't complain, Feverfew, you'll get these horse droppings; and for you, eager Phlox, I'll scatter this brown straw.

Why do you turn your noses up, people? Do you not like the way I smell?

*

Just a wee bit longer and we will do our garden one last good turn. We will let one or two more autumn frosts come and then we will make a bed for it out of green brushwood. We will bend the Roses and earth them up to the necks, we will load up the fragrant Spruce branches, and then good night. Usually, one covers all sorts of other things with this brushwood, such as a pocketknife or a smoker's pipe. At the beginning of spring, when we take the brushwood away, we shall meet with everything again.

But we are not out yet, we have not stopped flowering yet; the All Souls' *Aster* blinks its lilac eyes, the Primrose and Violet bloom as a sign that even in November it is spring, the Indian Chrysanthemum (so-called because it is not from India but from China) does not let any meteorological or political conditions, however bad, stop it from producing its whole, fragile, immense wealth of flowers, its carrot-red, dazzling white, golden and russet flowers; and the Rose still ushers its last blooms. Queen, you have been flowering for six months; you are certainly duty bound to your position.

And then, the leaves are still flowering: yellow, autumnal leaves and purple ones, rusty red ones, orange, paprika-red and blood-brown ones; and red, orange, black and hoary blue berries; and the yellow, reddish, pale wood of the bare twigs; and we are still not done. And even when they get snowed up, there will still be the dark-green Holly with its glowing, red fruit and the black Pine trees and the Cypresses and the Yews; there is never an end to it.

I tell you, there is no such thing as death; there is not even such a thing as sleep. We merely grow from one season to another. We must be patient with life, for it is eternal.

*

But even you who do not rule over the odd flowerbed of your own soil in the universe can pay homage to nature at this autumntime, namely, by planting Hyacinth and Tulip bulbs in flowerpots so that they will either freeze in the winter or bloom. One goes about it like this: you buy the relevant bulbs and a bag of nice compost from the nearest garden centre; after which, you look out all your old flowerpots in the cellar and attic and put a bulb in each one. Towards the end, you find that you have still got some bulbs but no flowerpots. So, you buy more flowerpots, whereupon

you discover that you have not got any bulbs left now but you have got a surfeit of flowerpots and soil. Then you buy a few more bulbs, but because you have not got enough soil again you buy a new bag of compost. Then you have got soil left over, which of course you do not want to throw away, and instead you buy some more flowerpots and bulbs. You carry on like this until the people at home forbid you any longer. Then you fill the windows, tables, cabinets, pantry, cellar and loft with them and look forward to the approaching winter with confidence.

PREPARATION

Why talk about it? All the indications are here now that nature, as we say, is turning in for its winter sleep. Leaf after leaf drops from my Birch trees with a motion at once beautiful and sad; what has flowered, withdraws into the earth; of what ran rampant, only a bare broom or a dripping stalk remains, a shrivelled dwindling or a dry stem; and the soil itself has a rotten smell of decay. Why talk about it? It is over for this year. *Chrysanthemum*, don't deceive yourself about the richness of life; little, white Cinquefoil, don't mistake this last sunshine for the ebullient sunshine of March. There's nothing that can be done, children, the party's over now; have a good winter sleep.

But not at all! Not at all! What has got into you? Don't give me that! What sort of sleep do you call this? Every year we say that nature is turning in for its winter sleep; but we have not looked at this sleep up close yet; or, more precisely, we have not looked at it yet from underneath. Let us turn things legs about head to know them better; let us turn nature legs about head to see into it; let us turn it roots about head. My

151

God, so this is sleep? You call this rest? One ought to say that vegetation has stopped growing upwards because it has not got time; for it has rolled up its sleeves and is growing downwards; it has spat into its palms and is digging itself into the ground. Look here, these pale things in the ground are new roots; look how far they are pushing out; one, two, three, heave! one, two, three, heave! Can you not hear the earth cracking with the furious, collective onslaught? I dutifully report, general, that phalanxes of roots have fought their way deep into enemy territory; the advance guards of the Phloxes have already made contact with the advance guards of the Bellflowers. Right you are, right; have them dig in in the captured territory, then; mission accomplished.

And these fat, white, fragile things here are new shoots and sprouts. Look how many there are; how surreptitiously you have spread, you faded, dried-out perennial, how you feel, how you are overflowing with life! You call this sleep? The devil take leaves and flowers, what a fuss! Here below, here underground the real work is taking place; here, here and here new stems are growing; from here to there, from within these November confines, March life will sprout forth; here underground the great programme of the spring is being mapped out. There has not been a moment's rest. Hey, here is the construction plan, here the foundations have been dug and the pipes laid. And we shall dig even further before the frost hardens the soil. Let spring build its green vaults on the pioneering work of

152

autumn. We, the forces of autumn, have done our bit.

A tough, plump bud underground, a tumour on top of a bulb, a strange outgrowth under the heels of dried-out leaves: a bomb out of which spring flowers will erupt. We say that spring is the time for germination; in fact, the time for germination is autumn. When we look at nature, it is true that autumn is the end of the year, but it is almost truer that autumn is the beginning of the year. It is a common view that leaves drop off in autumn and I really cannot dispute this; I would only argue that in a certain, deeper sense autumn is the time when leaves actually sprout. Leaves shrivel up because winter is approaching but they also shrivel up because spring is approaching, because new buds are being formed, small like explosive caps, out of which the spring will explode. It is an optical illusion that trees and bushes are bare in autumn; in fact, they are dotted with everything which will unwrap itself in early spring and open out. It is just an optical illusion that flowers perish in the autumn; for, really, they are being born. We say that nature is resting, whereas it is pushing ahead like mad. It has merely shut up shop and pulled the blinds; but, behind them, it is already unwrapping its new wares and filling its shelves to the point of sagging. Folks, this is the real spring; what is not done now will not be done in April either. The future is not ahead of us, for it is already here in the shape of a shoot, it is already among us, and what is not among us now will not be in the future either. We do not see

153

the shoots because they are underground, we do not know the future because it is within us. It sometimes seems to us as though we reek of decay, littered with dry remnants of the past, but if we could see what fat, white shoots are blazing a trail through this old, cultivated soil which we call today, what seeds are secretly sprouting, what old seedlings are rallying themselves and concentrating themselves into a living shoot which will one day sprout forth into flowering life, if we could see the secret bustling of the future among us, we would certainly say that our nostalgia and our misgivings are a load of rot, and that best of all is to be a living person, that is, a person who grows.

THE GARDENER'S DECEMBER

To be sure, everything really is finished now. Until now, he has dug, hoed and loosened, turned over, manured and added lime, mixed peat, ash and soot into the soil, pruned, sown, planted, transplanted, divided, put bulbs into the ground and taken tubers out for the winter, watered and wet, mown the grass, weeded, covered the plants with brushwood or earthed them up to the necks; all of this he has done from February to December, and not until now, when his garden is snowed under, does he remember that he has forgotten to do something: to look at it. For you should know that he has not had a moment to spare. When he was hurrying to look at a flowering Gentian in the summer, he had to stop in his tracks to pull a weed up out of the grass. When he had wanted to relish the beauty of the blooming Delphiniums, he found that they needed staking. When his Asters were coming into bloom, he rushed for a can to water them. When his Phlox was flowering, he pulled out some Couch-grass; when his Roses were blooming, he looked to see where to cut off suckers or treat mildew; when his Chrysanthemums

were flowering, he pounced on them with a hoe to loosen the compacted soil around them. What do you expect? There was always something that needed doing. Do you think that you can just thrust your hands into your pockets and have a gander at how it is looking?

Praise God, everything really is finished now; there may be the odd thing left to do; there at the back the soil is like lead, and I had wanted to move this Knapweed, but God rest you, the snow has already fallen. Gardener, why not go and have a look at your garden for the first time?

Well, this black thing sticking out of the snow is a russet *Viscaria*; this dead stalk is a blue Columbine;

157

and this clump of singed leaves is an *Astilbe*. And well, well, that broom over there is *Aster ericoides* and this, which is barely anything at all, is an orange Globeflower, and this little pile of snow is a *Dianthus*, of course it is a *Dianthus*. And that stalk over there is perhaps a red Tansy.

Brr, it is cold! Not even in the winter can one savour one's garden.

*

Well, fine, so light me a fire. Let us leave the garden to sleep under its light quilt of snow. It is good to think about other things, too. We have got a table full of unread books; let us get stuck into those. We have got so many other plans and worries; let us start on those. But have we covered everything properly with brushwood? Have we given the Redhot Poker enough cover? Did we not forget to cover the *Plumbago*? And the *Kalmia* needs to be shielded with a branch. Will our *Azalea* not freeze? What if our Asian Crowfoot bulbs do not come up? In that case, we can plant them over with... hang on... Hang on, let us have a look in one of these price lists.

So, the garden in December mainly resides in a large quantity of gardening catalogues. The gardener himself hibernates under glass in a heated room, tucked up to the neck not in manure or brushwood, but in gardening price lists and brochures, books and pamphlets, from which he learns:

158

1. that the most prized, rewarding and utterly indispensable plants are those which he has not yet got in his garden;

2. that everything which he has got is 'rather delicate' and 'apt to die from frost'; or that in one flowerbed he has planted a plant 'which requires moisture' next to a plant 'which needs to be shielded from

moisture'; that the one which he planted with especial care in fullest sun requires 'full shade' and vice versa;

3. that there are three hundred and seventy or more plant varieties which 'deserve more attention' and 'should not be missing from any garden' or which are at least 'an entirely new, striking variety, far surpassing previous results'.

Because of all of this, the gardener in December is usually very glum. For one thing, he starts to worry that not one of his plants will come up in the spring because of frost or mugginess, damp, drought, sun and lack of sun; and so he broods about how to fill the terrible gaps.

For another, he discovers that even if as little as possible dies, his garden will still not have almost any of those 'most prized, richly flowering, entirely new, unsurpassable' varieties which he has just read about in sixty catalogues; and this certainly leaves an unbearable gap which somehow has to be filled. At this point, the hibernating gardener loses all interest in what he has got in his garden, being fully occupied instead with what he has not got, which is, of course, far more. He pounces on his catalogues and ticks off what he has got to order, what, by God, must not go missing from his garden anymore. At the first go, he ticks off four hundred and ninety perennials which, cost what they may, he must order. When he tots them up, he cools off a bit and, with a bleeding heart, begins to cross out the ones which he will forego this time. He has to conduct this painful act of elimination another five times until he is left with only about a hundred and twenty of the 'most beautiful, most rewarding, most indispensable' perennials which — borne aloft with resounding joy — he orders right away. 'Send me them at the beginning of March!!' — God, if only it were March already, he thinks to himself, shivering with impatience.

Well, God has blinded him. In March, he will discover that with the utmost effort he will be able to find barely two or three spaces in his garden where he can plant anything else, and even then only by the fence, behind the Japanese Quince bushes.

*

When he has done this important and — as is clear — rather hasty winter work, the gardener starts to be bored beyond measure. Because 'it will begin in March', he counts the days to March, and since there are so many of them, subtracts fifteen days because 'sometimes it will begin in February'. It cannot be helped, one has to wait. So, the gardener pounces on something else, such as a sofa, settee or chaise longue, and has a try at nature's winter sleep.

Half an hour later, he flies up from this poised position, inspired by a new idea. Flowerpots! Why, flowers can be grown in flowerpots! All at once, thickets of Palm trees and Latanias appear before his eyes, Dragon Trees and Spiderworts, Asparagus Ferns, Kaffir Lilies, Aspidistras, Mimosas and Begonias in all their

161

tropical beauty; and among them, as we know, the odd, swift *Primula* and Hyacinth and *Cyclamen* will bloom. We will turn the hallway into an equatorial jungle, hanging tendrils will flow across the stairs, and in the windows we will put plants which will bloom like mad. So, now the gardener casts a quick glance about him; he no longer sees the room which he is occupying but the paradisiacal, virgin forest which he is going to create here, and he rushes to the nursery round the corner and brings back a complete armful of the treasures of the plant kingdom.

Bringing home as much as he can carry, he finds:

that when he puts it all together it does not look one jot like an equatorial, virgin forest but more like a small, potter's shop;

that he cannot put anything in the windows because — as the ladies of the house fanatically insist — windows are meant for ventilation;

that he cannot put anything on the stairs because it apparently makes them muddy and splashed with water;

that he cannot turn his hallway into a tropical, virgin forest because, despite his doleful pleas and curses, the ladies cannot be dissuaded from opening the windows onto the frosty air.

So, our garden man takes his treasures off to the cellar where, as he comforts himself, at least it will not freeze; and in early spring, poking about in the tepid soil outside, he will forget all about them. Which experience will not deter him one jot from trying again the following December to turn his abode into a winter garden with new flowerpots. In this, you may see the everlasting life of nature.

ON THE GARDENING LIFE

It is said that time brings Roses; this is true — usually one has to wait until June or July for Roses; and as for their growth, three years are enough for your Rose to form quite a decent crown of flowers. Far better would be to say that time brings Oak trees or that time brings Birches. I planted several little Birch trees, saying, 'There'll be a Birch grove here and in the corner here there'll stand a mighty, hundred-year-old Oak.' I planted a little Oak too, but two years have already passed and it is still not a mighty, hundred-year-old Oak tree and those Birch trees are still not a hundred-year-old Birch grove in which nymphs could dance. Fair enough, I will wait a few years more; we gardeners are immensely patient. I have got a Cedar of Lebanon in my lawn almost as tall as me. According to expert authority a Cedar should grow to a height of three hundred feet and a width of fifty feet. Well, I should like to live to see it reach its prescribed height and width; really, it would be only right and proper for me to be able to live this long in good health and, so to speak, reap the fruit of my labours. So far, it has grown a good ten inches. Fine, I will wait a bit more.

Take a bit of grass; it may, if you sow it properly and the sparrows do not peck it up, sprout in a fortnight, and you will have to cut it in six weeks' time, but it is still not an English lawn. I know an excellent recipe for the English lawn which — similar to the recipe for Worcestershire Sauce — comes 'from an English country gentleman'. An American multimillionaire said to this nobleman: 'Sir, I'll pay you whatever you want if you'll disclose to me how one makes such a perfect, green, dense, immaculate, velvet, uniform, lush, indestructible, in short, such an English lawn, as yours.' 'It's quite simple,' said the English country gentleman in reply. 'The soil has to be prepared well and deep; it has to be fertile and permeable, not acid or greasy or heavy or barren; then, it has to be levelled well so that it's like a table-top; then, you sow the grass seed and roll the earth carefully; then, you water it daily, and when the grass grows you mow it week after week, you sweep up the cuttings with a broom and roll the lawn; you have to spray it daily, water it, wet it, hose it or sprinkle it; and if you do this for three hundred years, you will have just as good a lawn as me.'

To this, you must add that every one of us gardeners would like, and in practice really ought, to try every type of Rose from the point of view of its buds and flowers, stems and foliage, coronas and other features; likewise, every type of Tulip and Lily, *Iris*, *Delphinium*, Carnation, Bellflower, *Astilbe*, Violet, Phlox, *Chrysanthemum*, *Dahlia*, *Gladiolus*, Peony, *Aster*, *Primula*, *Anemone*, Columbine, Saxifrage, Gentian, Sunflower, Daylily,

166

Poppy, Goldenrod, Globeflower and Speedwell, each of which has at least a dozen best and most indispensable variants, varieties and hybrids. In addition, one must include several hundred genera and species which have between only three and a dozen varieties. Plus, one must pay especial attention to alpine plants, aquatic plants, heathery, bulbous, ferny and shade-loving plants, woody plants and evergreens. If I were to tot it all up, I would get, at a very conservative estimate, to you, sir, so to speak, eleven hundred years. The gardener needs eleven hundred years to try, work through and in a practical way evaluate everything which appertains to him. I can't give it to you for less, unless I reduce it by five per cent because it's you and because perhaps you don't need to grow everything, although it's worth it; but you'll have to be quick and not lose a single day if you are going to manage everything that's necessary in the time. One must finish what one has begun; you are duty bound to your garden. I will not give you a rule for it; you must try for yourselves and stick at it.

We gardeners live somewhat for the future; if our Roses bloom, we think how much better they will bloom the following year; and in ten years or so this little Spruce will have grown into a tree — if only those ten years were already behind me! I would like to see what these Birch trees will be like in fifty years' time. The true, the best is ahead of us. Each successive year will add growth and beauty. Thank God that we will soon be another year on!

EXPLANATORY NOTES

Many people and many sources have helped me while I was writing this translation and its accompanying texts. I would, however, like to express my particular gratitude to Mrs. Alena Spurná, without whose goodwill, effort and talent this book would be a less satisfactory tribute to its original.

HOW A GARDENER COMES INTO BEING

p. 14 *A certain ripeness*: the Czech word for 'ripeness', 'zralost', also means 'maturity'. Čapek is playing with both meanings here. In the absence of one English word to convey both meanings, I have settled for 'ripeness' because it suggests 'maturity' more than 'maturity' does 'ripeness'. 'Ripeness' also preserves the extension of the metaphor from the previous paragraph.

p. 14 *you will be inflamed into becoming an ardent gardener*: again, Čapek is playing with two meanings of one Czech word. Literally, Čapek's original reads: 'you will become an inflamed [or 'ardent'] gardener', the Czech for 'inflamed', 'zanícený?', also meaning 'ardent'. There is a humorous allusion to the

Sleeping Beauty stories here, where the girl pricks her finger on a distaff and succumbs to an evil fairy's curse.

p. 16   *Pernetiana Roses*: in 1900, the French rose breeder Joseph Pernet-Ducher (1851-1928) bred the first bright yellow bedding rose. In 1910, he produced the red-yellow 'Soleil d'Or' and the true yellow 'Rayon d'Or'. These formed the basis of the Pernetiana group of roses.

THE GARDENER'S JANUARY

p. 20   *ice-flowers*: this is both an English and a Czech expression for ice patterns on the window.

SEEDS

p. 25   *the Elbe (but not from the Vltava)*: the river Vltava is a left-bank tributary of the Elbe. The confluence of the two rivers is at Mělník, north of Prague. The interconnection of the two rivers is part of Čapek's joke.

p. 25   *Walpurgis Night*: the Czech legend of 'noc filipojakubská' (St. Philip's and St. James's Night) is similar to that of the German Walpurgis Night, with which English readers may be familiar. On Walpurgis Night, the eve of May 1st (the date when the relics of St. Walburga (b. Wessex 710, d. 779) were moved to Eichstätt), witches are said to rendezvous in the Harz mountains. St. Philip's and St. James's feast day is on May 3rd. According to Czech legend, witches rendezvous in the Jeseník mountains in northern Moravia at this time (Moravia is one of the two main regions of the modern Czech Republic). Čapek invokes the legend here for its magical connotations.

THE GARDENER'S FEBRUARY

p. 31 Μηνιν αειδε, Θεα: Homer's *Iliad* begins 'Sing, goddess, of the cursed wrath of Achilles'.

p. 31 *paint for the trees*: in the Czech lands, the bases of the trunks of fruit trees are often painted with a lime preparation to protect them against pests and extreme temperature changes caused by strong spring sunshine.

p. 35 *into new sap*: Čapek is toying with two meanings of one Czech word. The Czech word 'míza' means 'sap' but, when used colloquially, also means 'a lease of life'.

ON THE ART OF GARDENING

p. 38 '*add even only one cubit to his stature*': Matthew 6.27 and Luke 12.25: 'And which of you by being anxious can add one cubit to his stature?' (RSV)

p. 44 The catalogues lying by the gardener's bed are price lists for perennials and flowers.

THE GARDENER'S MARCH

p. 46 *St. Matthias*: Western feast day February 24th.

p. 46 *St. Joseph*: St. Joseph of Arimathea's Western feast day is March 17th. The feast day of St. Joseph, the husband of Mary, Jesus's mother, is March 19th.

p. 46 *Jack Frost*: in Czech, 'the three ice-men'.

p. 46 *St. Swithin's Day*: Čapek's text reads 'Médard's hood'.

171

St. Médard's Day (June 8th) has the same significance for Czechs and some other nations as St.
Swithin's Day (July 15th) for the British. Traditionally,
if it rains on St. Swithin's Day, it will rain for forty
days: 'St. Swithin's Day, if it do rain, /For forty days it
will remain. /St. Swithin's Day, an it be fair, /For forty
days 't will rain nae mair.' The Czech version of the
St. Médard's Day tradition is that if it rains on this
day, figuratively, Médard's hood will drip for forty
days.

p. 46　*St. John of Nepomuk's Night*: May 16th.

p. 46　*St. Peter's and St. Paul's*: in the Roman Catholic
calendar there are five festivals of St. Peter and St.
Paul. The principal festival is on June 29th.

p. 46　*St. Methodius's and St. Cyril's*: Western feast day
February 14th.

p. 46　*St. Wenceslas's*: September 28th.

p. 48　*St. Joseph's Day*: see above.

p. 47　The calendar reads March 25th.

BUDS

p. 52　*Benešov*: a town twenty-five miles south of the Czech
capital, Prague.

THE GARDENER'S APRIL

p. 54　*a monster under whose hooves the grass will not
grow*: this is one of Čapek's favourite phrases. It may
not have one specific origin. Its meaning, however, is
clear. Hooves suggest a clumsy bestiality and perhaps even a devilish quality. The symbolism of both

172

hooves and grass may also derive something from Biblical symbolism where grass symbolises life, fertility and fragile mortality, and where uncloven hooves are a mark of uncleanness.

FESTIVAL

p. 63   The festival is Labour Day (in Czech, literally 'Festival of Labour' or 'Festival of Work'), on May 1st. Labour Day was celebrated in Čapek's time, was made much of in communist Czechoslovakia, and is still a public holiday in the Czech Republic today.

p. 65   *smoked meat and peas*: smoked meat and mashed peas are a staple food. They are often served to Czech children in school canteens.

p. 65   *I asked someone who had visited the late lamented Tolstoy*: this 'someone' is Tomáš Garrigue Masaryk, the first President of the Czechoslovak Republic. Masaryk's three meetings with Tolstoy are recounted in Čapek's *Talks with T. G. Masaryk* (1928-35). In the *Talks*, Masaryk recalls seeing Tolstoy's badly stitched boots at their first meeting, in Moscow. At the second meeting, at Yasnaya Polyana, Masaryk rebukes Tolstoy: 'To stitch your own boots and go on foot instead of travel by train; it's just a waste of time. What better things you could have done with the time!'

BLESSED RAIN

p. 77   *Letná*: an arid plain in Prague with views across the river Vltava to Prague's Old Town. Part of Letná was irrigated to allow a park to be laid out there in 1859-60. In later years, a huge monument to Stalin was erected here.

p. 77   *Kolín*: a town thirty miles east of Prague.

p. 77   *Prague*: the capital of the Czechoslovak Republic and of the Czech Republic today.

THE GARDENER'S JUNE

p. 81   *scythes*: these are still familiar implements in the Czech countryside. They are commonly used in mountain regions, on grass verges and in awkwardly accessible areas. Domestically, they are sometimes used in gardens where, for example, rabbits are reared for their meat.

p. 83   *sickle*: this is still a familiar gardening tool in the Czech Republic. The sickle is an important symbol in Czech culture. The root of the Czech word for 'August', 'srpen', is 'srp', meaning 'sickle'.

p. 84   *This is a sort of a thing on wheels*: cylinder lawn mowers had been in existence for a century when Čapek wrote *The Gardener's Year*. In the Czechoslovak Republic, they generally only seem to have been owned by wealthier, middle-class Czechs. This partly explains the excitement which Čapek describes 'when a lawn mower comes into a home.' Domestic lawn mowers are still uncommon in the Czech Republic because of their high cost (equivalent to a month's good salary) and because of the rarity in the Czech Republic of English-style lawns and

174

English-style, 'aesthetic' gardening, the preference, as in Čapek's day, being for gardens and plots to be used to grow home produce.

ON VEGETABLE GROWERS

p. 91   *Kohlrabies*: the kohlrabi is a popular vegetable in the Czech diet, as is cabbage.

p. 92   *Mary, Mary may be quite contrary...*: this is not a literal translation, Čapek's original relying on an inversion of a Czech idiom. Literally, Čapek's original reads: 'A goat may become a gardener, but a gardener would be hard-pressed to become a goat to munch his garden'. The Czech idiom 'to make a goat a gardener' means the same as the English 'to set a wolf to mind the sheep'.

p. 93   *Canaanite*: figuratively, Canaan is a land of promise because it was identified in the Bible as the land promised to the Israelites by God.

THE GARDENER'S JULY

p. 95   *Hussite*: Hussites held religious beliefs based on the teachings of the Czech religious reformer Jan Hus (c. 1370-1415). They were also often motivated by a belief that Hus wanted greater Czech self-determination. After Hus had been burned as a heretic in 1415, the Hussites fought against the Catholic Church and the Holy Roman Empire. Jan Žižka was a particularly successful leader of the Hussite army. Religious freedom for the Hussites was eventually guaranteed by Rome in the mid-1430s.

p. 96 *American stove*: probably chosen for its exoticism. Cast iron stoves were produced in large quantities in America after about 1728. America may also have obvious connotations of special discovery: in Czech, 'to discover America' ('objevit Ameriku') means 'to be a proper Columbus'. Čapek was interested in, and wrote about, many inventions, including the American coke stove.

p. 96 *Attila's grave*: Attila was king of the Huns from 434 to 453. Those who buried him and his treasure were murdered so that the location of his grave would never be known.

p. 96 *Sibylline Books*: in Greek legend, Sibyl was a prophetess and the Sibylline Books were a collection of prophecies. The Books were supposedly offered by the Cumaean sibyl to Tarquinius Superbus, the last of the kings of Rome. When Tarquinius Superbus refused to pay the asking price, the sibyl burned six volumes and sold the remaining three to him for the original price.

p. 99 *in a pickle — even in a tart and spicy pickle*: in Czech, literally, 'in an oven — even in a white-hot and glowing oven'. Playing with the idiomatic and literal meanings of words and phrases is one of Čapek's favourite comic devices.

p. 100 *Engliš's resignation*: Karel Engliš (1880-1961) was an economist, politician, philosopher, university professor, Minister of Finance (1920-21, 1925-28, 1929-31) and Governor of the Czechoslovak National Bank (1934-39). In July 1928 he tendered his resignation — but did not actually resign — as Minister of Finance. During his career, Engliš tendered his resignation several times. Indeed, in the words of his biographer, J. Kolařík, he was 'chronically prone to resignations.'

A BOTANICAL CHAPTER

p. 105 *Communist*: the Communist Party of Czechoslovakia (KSČ) was formed in 1921 by the breakaway, Marxist wing of the Social Democratic Party (itself formed in 1878) which had led workers in a general strike in 1920. Throughout the remaining years of the Czechoslovak Republic the KSČ was one of the strongest political parties, though it did not take part in any of the Republic's governing coalitions. Čapek was robustly anti-communist and published an essay "Why I Am Not a Communist" in 1924. This essay was later republished in *On Common Things* or, *Zóon Politikon* (1932).

p. 105 *Popular Party*: the Czech and Slovak Popular parties were both largely centre-right, Catholic-clerical parties.

THE GARDENER'S AUGUST

p. 112 *Gerlachovka*: at 8,737 feet, Gerlach peak is the highest summit in the Slovak Republic's High Tatras (mountains). Slovakia was part of the newly formed Czechoslovak Republic.

177

THE GARDENER'S SEPTEMBER

p. 119 *Cybele*: also known as the Great Mother of the Gods and by other names. Cybele was worshipped by the ancient Greeks and Romans as the mother of, and, therefore, giver of life to, the gods, human beings, animals and wild nature. Her lover was the fertility god, Attis.

p. 122 *'Herriot'*: presumably chosen because Édouard Herriot (1872-1957) had twice been French premier when Čapek wrote *The Gardener's Year* (and would be once more, in 1932) and because the rose 'Mme. Édouard Herriot' had been bred by the great French rose breeder, Joseph Pernet-Ducher (see note to p. 16 and p. 135).

THE GARDENER'S OCTOBER

p. 135 *Frau Druschki*: the rose, 'Frau Karl Druschki', was bred in Germany in 1901 by Peter Lambert.

p. 135 *Mme. Herriot*: the rose, 'Mme. Édouard Herriot', was bred in France in 1913 by Joseph Pernet-Ducher.

p. 135 *Mme. Caroline Testout*: the rose, 'Mme. Caroline Testout', was bred in France in 1890 by Joseph Pernet-Ducher.

p. 135 *Herr Wilhelm Kordes*: the rose, 'Wilhelm Kordes', was bred in Germany in 1922 by Wilhelm Kordes.

p. 135 *M. Pernet*: presumably M. Joseph Pernet-Ducher. There are countless roses with 'Pernet' in their name, the vast majority of them having been bred before Čapek wrote *The Gardener's Year* and many having been bred by Joseph Pernet-Ducher himself. Also see

178

the note to Pernetiana Roses p.16.

ON THE BEAUTIES OF AUTUMN

p. 139 *the souls of the dead*: this and the evocation of 'the smell of cemetery candles' allude to the Czech equivalent of All Souls' Day. Officially called Památka zesnulých ('Commemoration of the Deceased'), this day is more usually known as 'Dušičky', a diminutive and, therefore, affectionate form of the Czech word for 'souls', 'duše'. Dušičky is on November 2nd. On this day or the previous weekend, families clean family members' graves and decorate them with candles and flowers.

THE GARDENER'S NOVEMBER

p. 144 *vale of tears*: this is one of Čapek's favourite phrases. Its origin is 'the valley of Baca' in Psalm 84.6, sometimes translated as 'the vale of Weeping' or 'the vale of Tears'. Baca, as it seems to be meant in the Psalm, is a dry, sterile place which those 'whose strength is in God' make 'a place of springs'. If Čapek was familiar with the origin of the phrase, this may cast an even more humorous light on his several descriptions of the gardener trying to water his parched garden and even of him trying to irrigate it, in 'The Gardener's July', with his own sweat and spit.

p. 145 *Mr. Arne Novák*: (1880-1939). A Czech literary critic, literary historian and essayist. Čapek and Novák became friends, although Čapek criticised Novák for his traditionalism in his 1913 article 'Tradition and

179

Development! Presumably, this sense of Novák's conservatism and Novák's rising pre-eminence as a historian of Czech literature explain why Čapek chose to mention Novák here in connection with roots.

p. 145 *Mr. Zdeněk Nejedlý*: (1878-1962). A Czech musicologist, historian and politician. Nejedlý became a communist in the 1920s and joined the Communist Party in 1929. He took part in the communist coup d'état in 1948 and held several important government positions. He was an ideologue of communist interpretations of history, culture and the arts and a devotee of Hussitism and Czech folk traditions. Čapek may associate him with 'uprooting' because of his communist beliefs and/or because of his dislike of certain tendencies in Czech history and culture (for example, Nejedlý famously criticised the great Czech composer, Antonín Dvořák, whose compositions he considered too 'international').

p. 147 *Mme. Herriot*: see note to p.135.

p. 148 *Queen*: this address of the rose as a fairy tale-like character may have a stronger resonance with Czech readers than with British, fairy tales being more popular in the Czech lands than in Britain. Čapek also wrote fairy tales, some of them set in royal palaces.

THE GARDENER'S DECEMBER

p. 159 The gardener is surrounded with catalogues and price lists for roses, flowers, perennials and bulbs.

ON THE GARDENING LIFE

p. 165 *time brings Roses*: a Czech proverb, the actual proverb being 'Patience brings roses'.

p. 166 *an English lawn*: the notion of the 'English lawn' as something characteristic of gardens and parks in Britain is still very common in the Czech Republic.

p. 166 *an excellent recipe...the recipe for*: Čapek uses the Czech word, 'recept', which means both 'a recipe' and 'a (general) rule'. See note to p. 167.

p. 166 *Worcestershire Sauce*: a form of this sauce is popular in the Czech Republic but is bitterer than British versions.

p. 166 *English country gentleman...American multimillionaire*: these characters are stock figures in Čapek's fictional imagination.

p. 167 *I will not give you a rule for this*: Again, Čapek uses the Czech word 'recept'. See note to p. 166.

AFTERWORD

Karel Čapek was a Czechoslovak author whose success coincided almost exactly with two glorious decades of Czech history between the two world wars. He was fondly regarded in his country at the time and is still fondly remembered today. His association with the golden era of the Czechoslovak Republic, as his country was then called, is partly a historical coincidence and partly due to his own very deliberate identification with the values and ambitions of his country at the time. Indeed, he may properly be said not only to have identified with these values and ambitions, and to have expressed them, but to have helped formulate them.

For three hundred years prior to the independent Czechoslovak Republic being formed in 1918, the Czech lands had been dominated by a foreign, Hapsburg power. During these three centuries, Czech culture, religious freedom, political independence and even the Czech language itself had been suppressed, with varying degrees of ferocity. The cultural foundations of the restoration of independence had been laid in large part by Czech historians, philologists, journalists, authors and composers. As a writer who was only twenty-eight when his country achieved political freedom, therefore, Čapek almost inevitably chose not only to pursue his own artistic ambitions, which themselves came to define much of the character of the new republic, but to take up the traditional mantle of the Czech author and contribute to the social, cultural and intellectual development of his country. It is for these reasons that he is identified so strongly with the golden era of the Czechoslovak Republic.

In his day, Čapek was most famous as a journalist and playwright, but he also wrote novels, short stories, essays, travel books, translations, children's books and poetry. His fame reached beyond the borders of the Czechoslovak Republic: his books were widely translated, his plays were performed on stages around the world, and he was fêted in several foreign countries.

Tragically, after only twenty years of independence, the Czech lands were once again subjugated — this time by the forces of Nazism and Communism — and the values which Čapek had epitomised and championed with such zest, authority, originality and charm were trodden underfoot. Čapek's own works were censored or banned. Now, however, the Czech lands have entered a second decade in a new era of political freedom (only the fourth in almost four hundred years) and Čapek's influence is free to be felt in his free country again.

*

The Gardener's Year is the product of Čapek's journalism. The idea for it was conceived in the autumn of 1927. The central structure of the book is a series of articles on the months of the gardening year. The first of these, 'The Gardener's December', was published on 27th November, 1927, in the Czechoslovak newspaper, *Lidové noviny*. The others were published in *Lidové noviny* between January and November, 1928. Interspersed between these monthly chapters is a collection of articles on gardening or seasonal themes. Of these, only three were written expressly for *The Gardener's Year*: 'How a Gardener Comes into Being', 'On Vegetable Growers' and 'On the Gardening Life'. The others, with the exception of 'On Cactus Growers', which was published in *Pestrý týden* in 1928, were written between 1925 and 1927 and were again published in *Lidové noviny*.

The Gardener's Year was first published as a book in 1929. Four Czech editions were published before Čapek's death in 1938; three more were published posthumously; a fourth posthumous edition was a censored edition of 1941; a fifth was published in 1947. In communist Czechoslovakia, the next edition, the tenth, was not published until 1957.

*

The Gardener's Year is both the fruit of one of Čapek's several private interests and of his sense of his responsibilities as a Czechoslovak author. Its theme is

185

most obviously the relationship between the gardener and his garden, but it is also much more than this. It is certainly more than what Čapek calls 'a gardening manual'. A previous Czechoslovak owner of a copy of the book which I now own inscribed it in London in October, 1941: 'Life is never so bad as not to be worth living.' One doubts whether the owner of a conventional gardening manual would feel so inspired by the book and so supported by it in dark times as to inscribe it with a similar statement.

One does, of course, in part read *The Gardener's Year* as a source of gardening instruction. Čapek's interest in gardening was thorough and his knowledge was broad. Like the gardener in *The Gardener's Year*, he created a garden of his own from scratch at a house which he built with his brother, Josef (whose drawings accompany his text), and this garden was much admired by friends like the author, František Langer. When his brother-in-law's brother later gave him the use of a country house near Dobříš as a wedding gift, Čapek also worked hard to turn the land into a park. (One can only imagine how he must have relished the woodlands, ponds, meadows and stream there which he jokes in 'The Gardener's August' that the amateur gardener longs to incorporate into his garden.) From the record of one of his other hobbies, photography, numerous photographs remain which Čapek took of his rockery, plants, trees, potted plants and cacti. And from reading *The Gardener's Year* one can see just how large his knowledge of plants was and how much of his knowledge of gardening must have come from experience and detailed observation.

The Gardener's Year, however, would not have been as popular as it has been and would not have served Čapek's sense of his larger responsibilities if it had not also taken far longer perspectives. The very type of gardening which Čapek describes in the book seems to aspire to a certain cultural development of his country. In his preference for 'aesthetic' gardens he is undoubtedly advocating an alternative to the more usual, Czech garden which, then as now, was planted to grow home produce or was intended for other, more practical purposes. In particular, he seems to be aspiring to a garden culture which comes nearer to those of wealthy, long-established and long-independent, foreign countries with their 'English lawns', French-bred roses and expensive garden machinery.

Such longer perspectives not only take Čapek to a view of the gardens of Europe and America but onwards still to a view of the very human condition. In the position of the amateur gardener Čapek seems to see in miniature much of the whole comedy of man. His amateur gardener represents an irrepressible tendency among men (women play less of a role in the comedy) to try to impose their will on nature and their fellow man, to try to control, direct, become authorities and anticipate nature; and, typically of such presumption, much of the comedy of the book lies in the recognition of man's arrogance, impotence and inevitable frustration. Indeed, though Čapek does not seem to have been Christian himself, his outlook reminds us of a Christian view of man as, far from being a master of nature, having actually been excluded from it. Several times in *The Gardener's Year* he describes man's physical inadequacies for the tasks of gardening. Several times he mentions the Garden of Eden, the paradise of nature from which man's mythical ancestors were expelled. And once he explains in detail the significance of this myth for the ignorance of man: Adam tried to pluck the unripe fruit of the Tree of Knowledge and from that time on, 'the fruit of the Tree of Knowledge has been, and always will be, unripe'.

Against the background of such ignorance and presumption, Čapek presents the related comedy of the large gulf — often more obvious to the observer than to the obsessive gardener — between the gardener's will and experience, and between his self-image and actual character and effect. True to Čapek's sense of the vanity of man, his amateur gardener is someone whose optimism and self-worth are more often products of his own will and fantasy than of the recognition and reasonable assessment of actual facts. His gardener is someone who tries to grow an 'equatorial jungle' indoors in the winter, who boasts of a plant being a rare hybrid only to find that it is just a horseradish, who uses his cunning to try to pass his unwanted grass on to an old lady or to buy a plant from a reluctant nurseryman (in both cases without the exactly desired result), and who is grossly unreasonable to a friend who is looking after his garden while he is away.

However, despite this sense of man's ignorance and presumption Čapek cannot be said to be dismissive of man. In his admission of the comic aspects of man's condition alone he shows an obvious affection for man (and, fittingly, his narrator is just as foolish as other gardening men). Indeed, while most of gardening man's follies can be seen to originate from an immodest will, Čapek shows us that man is also capable of an endearing innocence: in a passage which reminds us that not all men are like Adam, Čapek imagines how a gardener arriving at the Garden of Eden would notice that the Tree of Knowledge 'did not have a nice, bowl-shaped border fashioned round it' and how he would 'begin to fumble about in the soil, not even knowing what was hanging above his head'.

Nor does Čapek satirise man without suggesting an alternative to the follies which he satirises. In the very recognition of the contrast between man's will and experience, he is inevitably implying a solution. In fact, one may clearly see Čapek's attraction to the philosophy of Pragmatism in this solution (Čapek was a doctor of philosophy and published his *Pragmatism or, The Philosophy of the Practical Life* in 1918). True to the Pragmatic empiricism which sees truths, values and rightness as confirmed in the course of experience and, therefore, as being fallible and subject to revision, Čapek's gardener's folly is that he often pursues ideas

189

formed by his own will and imagination without properly referring them back to experience or revising them in the light of experience.

Čapek's actual faith in man, which is itself inherent in his Pragmatic philosophy, is also evident in the very large amount of implicit and explicit, gardening and non-gardening instruction which, for all his gentle mockery, he still feels it worth offering to his Czechoslovak readers in particular. One suspects from even quite recent attitudes to the Czech Festival of Work that his ideas in the chapter 'Festival' must have seemed original to the point of controversy. He draws lessons from nature which he must have felt were particularly suitable for his fledgling nation, such as reasons to be proud of what seemed especially 'Czech' (like sugar beet), or to be sure to make the right effort, or to be optimistic, or to value skill and expertise. Several positive assumptions of the book are recognisably Pragmatic, such as the belief in the importance of trying to improve conditions, of the need for action in the acquisition of knowledge, of experimentalism, of development, and of a pluralistic outlook. In a linguistic sense, his use of a large number of Czech, common plant names, his witty puns on Czech words and idioms, and his broad range of verbal effects and styles would all, in the context of Czech cultural history, have suggested to his Czechoslovak readers something of the potential of the Czech language and would have helped them feel a sense of pride in, and repossession of, their linguistic inheritance, just as

190

previous generations of Czech writers had tried to do. And in the huge frame of reference which he builds around his Czechoslovak gardener (Čapek draws on everything in *The Gardener's Year* from international politics to Czechoslovak social life to private fantasies), he helped his Czechoslovak readers feel an even greater sense of repossession: of their very membership of the human community.

Finally, though Čapek does mock a form of ignorant presumption, one of the abiding morals of the book, nevertheless, is Čapek's passionate encouragement of optimism and resolve. No doubt it is this lesson of the book, above all, which so appealed to the previous Czechoslovak owner of the copy of *The Gardener's Year* which I now own. Indeed, Čapek repeatedly cites reasons to be optimistic and he has no patience at all for the idle:

> 'Only those who have their hands in
> their pockets say that it is changing for
> the worse.'

From a Czechoslovak, national point of view, such encouragement of optimism and will, like Čapek's Pragmatism, is also stressed for its usefulness in the building of the new, Czechoslovak state. In Čapek's insistence that, despite many limitations upon man, there is still cause to be optimistic about what one can achieve, he is addressing not only a universal human possibility but a constant anxiety of Central Europeans whose fates have always been heavily influenced by the wills of neighbouring countries. (On a personal level, such determined optimism may also have helped Čapek in his own struggle against a crippling spinal disease which, among other hardships, prevented him from marrying Olga Scheinpflugová for over a decade). In common with other superficially Christian characteristics of the book, Čapek may even be said to suggest that there is a type of salvation available to the committed but restricted 'gardener': though nature does not always match the gardener's efforts or will with the exactly desired result, it can, nevertheless, through a combination of human will and natural process, offer the gardener the most glorious rewards for his faith and works. Crocuses and snowdrops may spring up in the garden without the gardener 'having an inkling' and without, in the immediate term, him 'having taken the least efforts towards it', but they spring up, nevertheless, because the gardener has prepared the soil for them and has sown seeds or planted bulbs. And in order to impress upon us the full splendour of this possible reward, Čapek draws on a huge verbal range, narrative skill and metaphorical creativity to try to depict nature's scale, diversity, beauty, change, virility and fragility.

In short, for all its lightness of touch, which is so characteristic of Čapek's works, *The Gardener's Year* is, just as characteristically, a profound book. For Čapek, gardening is both itself and an almost infinite metaphor for human life. *The Gardener's Year* is a picture of both the provincialism of man and of his position within the largest natural, psychological,

192

social, cultural and historical contexts. It is a picture which acknowledges these contexts implicitly and explicitly and which draws frequently very positive lessons from them both for Czechoslovaks and for man at large. It is a picture which, assisted by his artist brother, Josef's, drawings, Čapek creates with great intelligence, good humour and charm.

A Chronology of Karel Čapek

1890   9th January: Birth of Karel Čapek in Malé
        Svatoňovice, Bohemia.
1895   Begins school in Úpice.
1901-5 Studies at gymnázium (academic secondary
        school) in Hradec Králové. Is expelled for belong-
        ing to a patriotic student society.
1904   Publishes first poem.
1905   Studies at gymnázium in Brno.
1907   Family moves to Prague. Studies at gymnázium in
        Prague.
1909   Begins studies in Philosophy at Charles
        University, Prague.
1910   Studies at Friedrich Wilhelm University, Berlin.
1911   Studies at the Sorbonne, Paris. Begins to write
        Loupežník (The Brigand) with brother, Josef (b.
        1887).
1915   Becomes Doctor of Philosophy from Charles
        University, Prague.
1916   Publishes first book, *Zářivé hlubiny (The Shining
        Depths)*, which includes the play *Lásky hra osud-
        ná (Love's Fateful Game)*, written with Josef.
1917   Becomes a member of the editorial staff of the
        weekly, *Národ*.
        Publishes a collection of short stories, *Boží muka
        (The Wayside Cross)*. Joins the editorial staff of
        the newspaper, *Národní listy*.

1918   Publishes *Pragmatismus čili Filozofie praktického
        života (Pragmatism or, The Philosophy of the
        Practical Life)*. Publishes *Krakonošova zahrada
        (Krakonosh's Garden)*, a collection of prose writ-
        ings written with Josef.

1919   Translates poetry by Apollinaire.

1920   *Loupežník (The Brigand)* premieres at the National
        Theatre, Prague. Meets Olga Scheinpflugová, the
        daughter of a colleague at *Národní listy*. Publishes
        a collection of articles, *Kritika slov (A Critique of
        Words)*, and a play, *R.U.R.*

1921   *R.U.R.* premieres in Hradec Králové and later at
        the National Theatre, Prague. Publishes *Trapné
        povídky (Awkward Tales)*. Joins the editorial staff
        of the newspaper, *Lidové noviny*, with Josef.
        Becomes a producer at the Prague theatre,
        Městské divadlo Královských Vinohrad. Publishes
        the play *Ze života hmyzu (From the Life of Insects)*,
        written with Josef.

1922   *Ze života hmyzu (From the Life of Insects)*
        premieres at the National Theatre, Brno and later
        at the National Theatre, Prague. Meets President
        T. G. Masaryk for the first time when Masaryk
        visits the Vinohrady theatre. Publishes a novel,
        Továrna na Absolutno (A Factory for the Absolute).
        Věc Makropulos (The Makropoulos Affair)
        premieres at the Vinohrady theatre.

1923   *Ze života hmyzu (From the Life of Insects)* pre-
        mieres in Berlin. Čapek travels in Germany.
        Leaves his post at the Vinohrady theatre. Travels

to Italy. Publishes *Italské listy (Letters from Italy)*.

1924 Mother dies. Publishes a novel, *Krakatit*. Travels to Britain. Publishes *Anglické listy (Letters from England)*.

1925 Is nominated Chairman of the new Prague P.E.N. Publishes *Jak vzniká divadelní hra (How a Play Comes into Being)*. Publishes collection of articles, *O nejbližších věcech (On Intimate Things)*.

1927 *Adam Stvořitel (Adam the Creator)* premieres at the National Theatre, Prague. Publishes *Skandální aféra Josefa Holouška (The Disgraceful Scandal of Josef Holoušek)*.

1928 Publishes first part of *Hovory s T. G. Masarykem (Talks with T. G. Masaryk)*.

1929 Publishes *Povídky z jedné kapsy (Tales from One Pocket)*. Publishes *Zahradníkův rok (The Gardener's Year)*. Father dies. Travels to Spain. Publishes *Povídky z druhé kapsy (Tales from the Other Pocket)*.

1930 Publishes *Výlet do Španěl (A Trip to Hispania)*.

1931 Publishes second part of *Hovory s T. G. Masarykem (Talks with T. G. Masaryk)*. Travels in Holland. Publishes collection of literary essays, *Marsyas čili Na okraj literatury (Marsyas or, To the Margins of Literature)*. Publishes *Devatero pohádek (Nine Fairy Tales)*.

1932 Publishes *Apokryfy (Apocryphal Stories)*. Publishes *O věcech obecných čili Zóon politikon (On Common Things or, Zóon Politikon)*. Publishes *Obrázky z Holandska (Pictures from Holland)*.

Publishes *Dášeňka čili Život štěněte (Darshenyka or, The Life of a Puppy)*.

1933   Publishes first part of a novel trilogy, *Hordubal*. Resigns as Chairman of P.E.N.

1934   Publishes second part of the trilogy, *Povětroň (Meteor)*. Publishes third part of the trilogy, *Obyčejný život (An Ordinary Life)*.

1935   Publishes third part of *Hovory s T. G. Masarykem (Talks with T. G. Masaryk)*. Travels in the Dolomites with Olga Scheinpflugová. Marries Olga Scheinpflugová.

1936   Publishes novel, *Válka s Mloky (War with the Newts)*. Travels through Denmark, Sweden and Norway. The Norwegian press propose Čapek for the Nobel Prize for Literature. Publishes *Cesta na sever (A Journey to the North)*. Publishes *Jak se dělají noviny (How Newspapers Are Made)*.

Drawing of Karel Čapek by Adolf Hoffmeister, 1938

197

1937 *Bílá nemoc (The White Sickness)* premieres at the Estates Theatre, Prague, and then at the State Theatre, Brno. Travels through Austria, Switzerland and southern France. President Masaryk dies. Publishes novel, *První parta (The First Crew)*.

1938 *Matka (Mother)* premieres at the Estates Theatre, Prague. 25th December (6.45pm): Čapek dies. Leaves an unfinished novel, *Život a dílo skladatele Foltýna (The Life and Work of the Composer, Foltýn)*.

1968 Olga Scheinpflugová dies.

A Brief Chronology of Josef Čapek

1887   23rd March: Birth of Josef Čapek in Hronov,
        Bohemia.
1890   9th January: Birth of brother, Karel.
1904   Studies at the School for Applied Arts in Prague
        (until 1910).
1905   June: first joint exhibition in Prague.
1907   November: publication of a first named literary col-
        laboration with Karel in *The Moravian-Silesian
        Review*. Ultimately, Josef would write almost 1,500
        critical articles and reviews.
1909   First colour reproduction published in a magazine,
        Dílo (Work [of Art]).
1910   Writes first play with Karel, *Lásky hra osudná
        (Love's Fateful Game)*, published in 1911; first jour-
        ney to Paris (until July 1911); first encounter with
        Cubism.
1911   Editor of the magazine *Arts Monthly*.
1912   June: resigns as editor of *Arts Monthly*; second trip
        to Paris.
1913   Visits the Autumn Salon in Berlin.
1916   Graphic designs reproduced in the German expres-
        sionist magazine, *Die Aktion*.
1917   *Die Aktion* publishes an issue dedicated to Josef;
        takes part in an exhibition in Berlin organised by
        Die Aktion.
1918   Part-exhibits in Vienna; first linocut book cover;

199

Krakonošova zahrada (Krakonosh's Garden) pub-lished, a collection of Josef's and Karel's prose writ-ings from 1908-12; editor and art critic for the national newspaper *Národní listy*.

1920   Part-exhibits in a series of exhibitions in Germany, Austria and Switzerland; start of intensive work on book jackets, including designs for book covers for books by Karel. In all, Josef would design over five hundred book jackets.

1921   First design work for the theatre (advised on cos-tumes for the staging of Karel's play *R.U.R.*). In all, Josef would design the scenery for over fifty plays. Josef and Karel leave *Národní listy* and join anoth-er Czechoslovak newspaper, *Lidové noviny*.

1924   First solo exhibition in Prague; takes part in an exhibition of modern Czech art in Paris.

1927   Premiere of last play written with Karel, *Adam Stvořitel (Adam the Creator)*.

1928   *The Works of the Čapek Brothers* begins to be pub-lished.

1930   Takes part in an exhibition of One Hundred Years of Czech Art.

1932   Last design work for the theatre.

1933   Anti-fascist caricatures published in *Lidové noviny*.

1934   Solo exhibition in Brno; takes part in the anti-fas-cist International Exhibition of Humour and Caricature in Prague.

1937   Cycle of satirical, anti-Hitler drawings, *The Dictator's Boots*, published in *Lidové noviny*; takes part in an exhibition of modern Czechoslovak art in Paris and in the U.S.S.R.

1938 Series of anti-war caricatures, *Modern Times*, published in *Lidové noviny*; death of Karel.

1939 1st September: arrested and interned in Dachau concentration camp; 26th September: interned in Buchenwald concentration camp.

1942 26th June: transported to Sachsenhausen concentration camp.

1945 25th February: transported to Bergen-Belsen concentration camp; 4th April: last recorded sighting; 15th April: Bergen-Belsen liberated by British troops; 25th April: Josef reported missing, thought to have died during a typhus epidemic at Bergen-Belsen.

Josef Čapek in his studio (Photograph by F. Illek.)